GW01157702

A MOMENT IN TIME

FOREWORD BY SIR TOM FARMER CBE

WRITTEN BY JOHN STEPHENS & TOM WRIGHT

"A moment in life. A moment in time.
A moment in history. At last, at last. At last!
Hibs have won the Scottish Cup!"

IAN CROCKER, SKY SPORTS COMMENTATOR, 21 MAY 2016

A Moment in Time

Photographs © Cameron Allan, Stephen Dunn, Alan Rennie, SNS Group.

Foreword by Sir Tom Farmer CBE
Written by John Stephens & Tom Wright

A Grange Publication

© 2016. Published by Grange Communications Ltd., Edinburgh, under licence from Hibernian Football Club. Printed in the EU.

Every effort has been made to ensure the accuracy of information within this publication but the publishers cannot be held responsible for any errors or omissions. Views expressed are those of the author and do not necessarily represent those of the publishers or the football club. All rights reserved.

ISBN 978-1-911287-32-2

CONTENTS

Foreword	7
Looking Back – Hibernian's 1887 & 1902 Scottish Cup Victories	11
The Road to Hampden	15
The Semi Final	29
The Final	40
The Presentation	123
The Dressing Room	163
The Parade	175
114 Years Is No More	217

FOREWORD

BY SIR TOM FARMER CBE

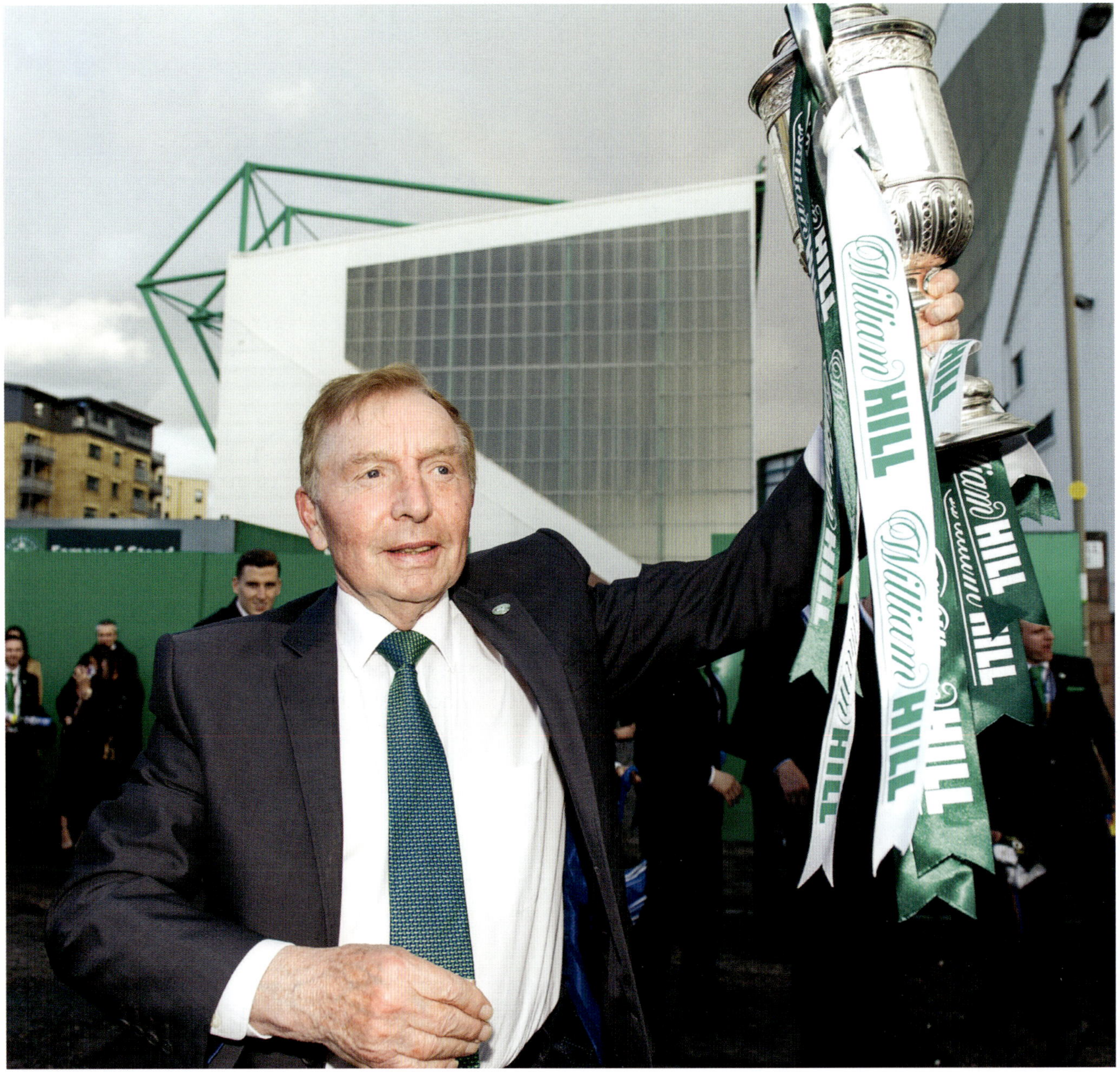
William HILL

FOREWORD, BY SIR TOM FARMER CBE

Martin Luther King the great leader of the American Civil Rights Movement in the 1960s gave a speech called "I have a dream" which became the defining moment in the history of that movement and its impact on the United States.

In a similar vein my dream was that one day that I would be involved with the Hibernian Football Club when it won the Scottish Cup, because 114 years ago in 1902 Hibernian also won the Cup when my grandfather John Farmer was a Director and his brother Philip, my uncle, was President. Indeed that day when they brought the cup back to Leith my grandfather took the cup home with him and placed it on the sideboard in his house. It was something in my family that was talked about quite often.

I never thought a tear would appear in my eye with the emotion but I couldn't believe it as I looked around me. There were 25,000 people, Hibs supporters, all crying tears of joy. I am not ashamed to say that I shed a tear as well. My grandson was sitting next to me at Hampden and he was hugging me and I turned to Rod Petrie, who also had tears in his eyes, and simply said, "they have done it".

It was a fantastic and emotional day that I will never forget and I am sure that no Hibernian supporter, regardless of whether they were at Hampden or not, will forget either.

I hope with this book of photographs supporters can relive some of the emotion and joy that was released when the final whistle went on that historic day. Saturday, 21 May 2016 is now enshrined in our Club's history and I know that there will be many more special days and victories to come.

This book is dedicated to all Hibernian supporters and to those supporters who are no longer with us but who I know will be looking down from heaven with a smile on their face. It is dedicated to those young and old, past and present, who persevered and longed for that moment in time. The moment Hibernian Football Club won the Scottish Cup.

LOOKING BACK – HIBERNIAN'S 1887 & 1902 SCOTTISH CUP VICTORIES

LOOKING BACK – HIBERNIAN'S 1887 & 1902 SCOTTISH CUP VICTORIES

Hibernian's first ever Scottish Cup tie ended in a 2-1 victory over local rivals Hearts on the East Meadows on 6 October 1877, after a replay, before eventually going down to Thornliebank in the fourth round.

During the following few seasons the club would regularly manage to reach the latter stages of the competition, but it was not until season 1883-84, when after again defeating rivals Hearts on the way, they finally reached the first of what would be three consecutive semi-finals. In 1887 they would go a step further by qualifying for the final itself.

After victories over Durhamtown Rangers, Mossend Swifts, Hearts, and Queen of the South Wanderers, a 2-1 victory over Third Lanark in Glasgow saw Hibernian reach their fourth consecutive semi-final, which in itself was a not inconsiderable feat. A 3-1 victory over Vale of Leven at the penultimate stage of the competition was enough to seal the Club's entry into the Scottish Cup final – or so it was thought. It was only after the game that it was discovered that an official letter of protest had been sent to the SFA by Vale of Leven claiming that the Edinburgh side had infringed the rules by fielding an ineligible player, Willie Groves, alleging that the Leith-born Groves was a professional player, which in those days was very much against the rules.

Hibernian now found themselves embroiled in a controversy that could well have cost them the Scottish Cup. The basis of the protest was that Hibernian had paid the 17 year old inside forward Groves, an apprentice stonemason to trade, more than just the accepted payment in lieu of time lost from work, indeed, according to evidence from a private investigator that had been paid to follow the player, up to four times more.

Somewhat ludicrously part of Vale's protest was that Groves and several other Hibernian players had partaken of breakfast and dinner in a local establishment, the meals paid for by the football club. Just days before the final against Dumbarton was due to take place an emergency meeting of the SFA committee called to investigate the matter, remained unresolved and another meeting was convened, but incredibly this would not take place until after the final itself had been played.

At that time Dumbarton were a strong and skilful side that had won the Scottish Cup just a few years before, and in the eyes of many had every right to be considered strong favourites to lift the cup for a second time. Their team contained several current Scottish internationals including the famous 'Prince of Goalkeepers' James McCauley and would prove to be formidable opponents.

On Saturday, 12 February 1887, the teams took the field at Second Hampden to contest the

14th Scottish Cup Final. Hibernian won the toss and allowed Dumbarton to kick off playing into a strong wind.

The treacherous underfoot conditions made good football difficult for both sides but the west coast side had the better of the early play, claiming a goal that was rightly chalked off on account of the ball going outside the goalposts, which at that time were still without nets. Although fiercely contested the game had provided little in the way of goalmouth action and the first half ended goalless.

The second half started much the same as the first with chances at a premium at either end, but on the hour mark Dumbarton took the lead when inside left Aitken fired a strong shot past Tobin in the Hibernian goal. Using the wind to their advantage the 'Sons' now appeared content to hang on to their slender lead, but not to be outdone, Hibernian started to take control of the game and Clark levelled things midway through the half much to the delight of the huge travelling support from Edinburgh.

With only a few minutes of the game remaining both sides reinforced their determination to settle the issue, but a great jinking run by Groves ended with Lafferty scoring Hibernian's second goal, despite Dumbarton's vain appeal for offside. It was the goal that would win Hibernian the Scottish Cup for the first time – or so they hoped.

After a celebratory dinner in the St Mary's Halls in the east end of Glasgow, the triumphant Hibernian players made their way to Queen Street Station for the return trip to Edinburgh. Back in the capital the result of the Scottish Cup Final had been received with tremendous excitement and a huge crowd was waiting at the Waverley Station to greet the victorious team on their arrival back in the city later that evening.

All the way up Waverley Bridge, along the east end of Princes Street into the North Bridge and finally down the High Street, the route was packed with jubilant crowds, many waving banners, before the players, led by a couple of bands, finally entered the Institute in St Mary's Street where the celebrations would go on well into the night.

The reconvened meeting to decide Vale's appeal and Hibernian's fate was yet to be held, and on the Tuesday, just three days after the final, Vale of Leven's protest went before the committee for a second time.

Both parties presented a strong case in a heated debate that went on for some time, but in the end the committee remained split down the middle with six voting for Hibernian, six against, the remainder undecided.

Another vote again failed to settle matters and it was left to the casting vote of the chairman who after some deliberation came down on the side of Hibernian, thereby officially confirming the Easter Road side as winners of the Scottish Cup for the very first time.

By the turn of the new century the astute Dan McMichael had assembled a side containing a mixture of youth and experience that was destined to take the club to new heights and they entered the 1901-02 Scottish Cup competition in high spirits.

A 2-0 victory against Rangers at Ibrox in the semi-final had set up an all-green cup final with Celtic. With work still taking place at the national stadium at Hampden, the final was originally to have taken place at Ibrox on Saturday, 12 April 1902.

Unfortunately, the tragic events during the Scotland-England game at the same ground seven days before, when 25 people had been killed and well over 500 injured after part of the flimsy wooden terracing behind one of the goals had collapsed, meant the final had been temporarily postponed. It was later decided that even although it was the home ground of one of the finalists, the game would now go ahead at Parkhead a few weeks later.

The teams took the field at Parkhead on Saturday, 26th April 1902. Celtic had now been installed as favourites, not only because of the distinct advantage of playing on home turf, but also because of their record in the competition, this being their fourth consecutive final, winning two of the previous three. At the kick off it was obvious that the gale force, swirling wind that was blowing from goalmouth to goalmouth would make good football difficult for both sides and spoil the game as a spectacle for the 16,000 fans that had packed into the ground.

With the wind at their back, somewhat predictably, Celtic were the more direct and dangerous team in the opening period, going close on several occasions as the Hibernian defence was forced to stand firm against the incessant pressure, the half ending goalless.

In the second period the Easter Road side started to use the blustery conditions to their advantage and looked the more likely to score. Continuing to assert themselves in the difficult conditions, Welsh cap Bobby Atherton thought he had opened the scoring only for the goal to be disallowed for offside. A goal was not long in coming however, and when it did arrive it would be in favour of the Edinburgh side.

Callaghan took a corner on the right, and according to legend, Atherton's shout for a Celtic defender to 'leave it' allowed the tricky McGeachan to take advantage of the situation by cheekily back-heeling the ball into the net. Disputed or not, it was the goal that would decide the cup final.

At a short ceremony in the Alexander Hotel in Glasgow, the Hibernian President, Phillip Farmer, was presented with the trophy before the victorious side made their way to Queen Street Station for the trip back to Edinburgh.

Arrangements had been made for the Hibernian party to disembark at Haymarket where they were met by a huge crowd, the rousing music of a brass band, and a carriage waiting to transport the triumphant players and officials on their victory parade along Princes Street, down Leith Street and along London Road to the ground. Everywhere the route was crammed with jubilant supporters, the traffic brought to a grinding halt at the bottleneck of the North Bridge and Waterloo Place by a mass of excited bodies, all aware of what a momentous occasion it was for the city. Later the celebrations would continue long into the night.

The following season the nucleus of the cup winning side would help the club to win the First Division Championship for the first time, however the jubilant Hibernian fans that had welcomed the triumphant cup winning side back to Edinburgh in 1902 were not to know it at the time, but it would be another 114 years before a Scottish Cup success would again be celebrated in the east side of the city.

THE ROAD TO HAMPDEN

"I just feel that we had the edge.

If it had went to a fight, we would have won it.

If it had went to a game of football,

we would have won it."

KEVIN THOMSON

16 | A MOMENT IN TIME

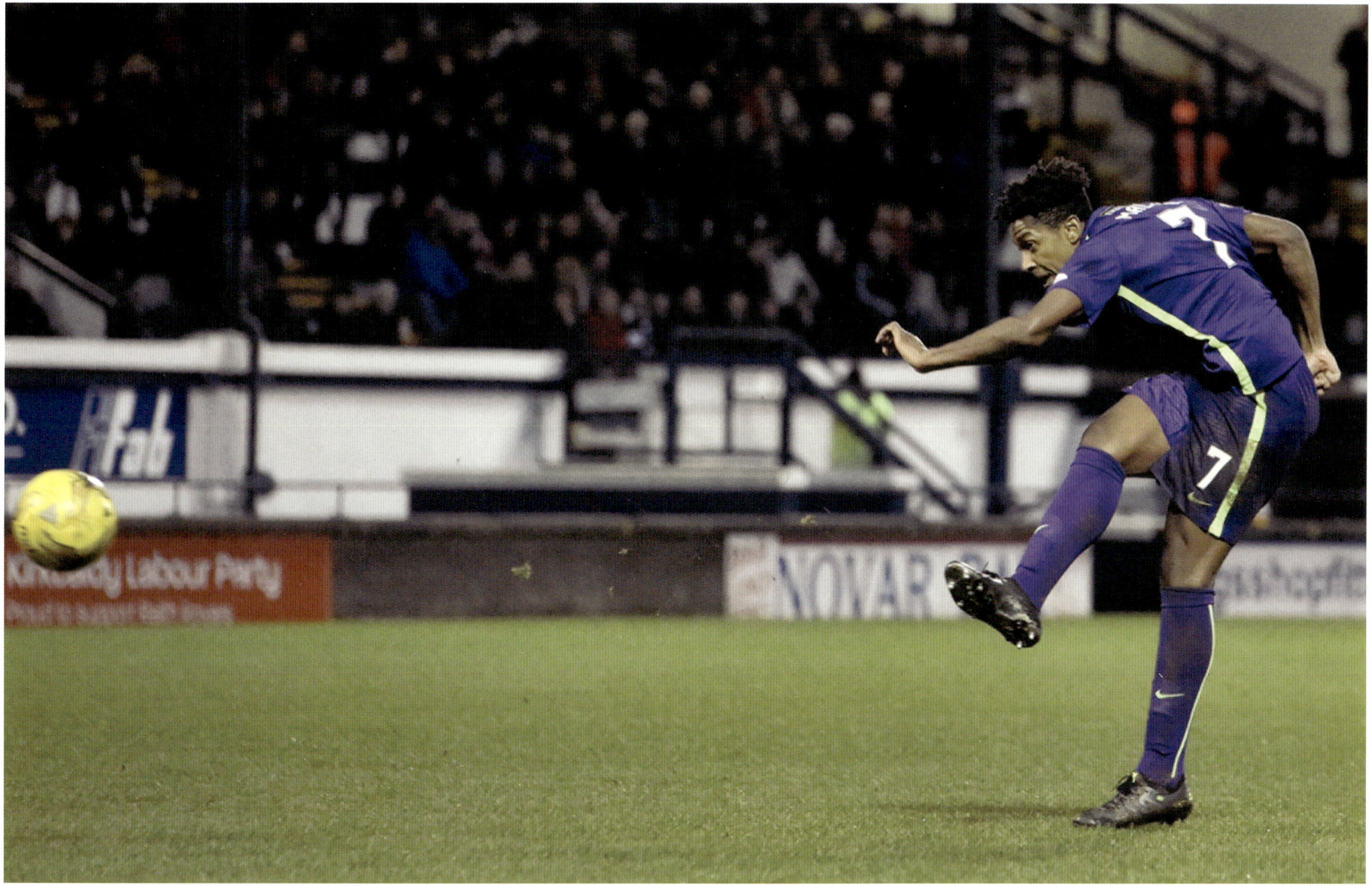
Kirkcaldy Labour Party

William Hill Scottish Cup Fourth Round: Raith Rovers 0-2 Hibernian; D. McGregor, D. Malonga

ont-group.co.uk
Hepburn
EMSLIE
0131 551 5611
WELDING · MACHINING
MECHANICAL · STRUCTURAL
0131 551 5670
OHN ROBERTSON LOUNGE
TO BOOK CALL
0131 200 7205
01383 921 187
CHEERS BARS
williamhill

William Hill Scottish Cup Fifth Round: Heart of Midlothian 2-2 Hibernian; A. Djoum, S. Nicholson; J. Cummings, P. Hanlon

A MOMENT IN TIME | 21

22 | A MOMENT IN TIME

William Hill Scottish Cup Fifth Round Replay: Hibernian 1-0 Heart of Midlothian; J. Cummings.

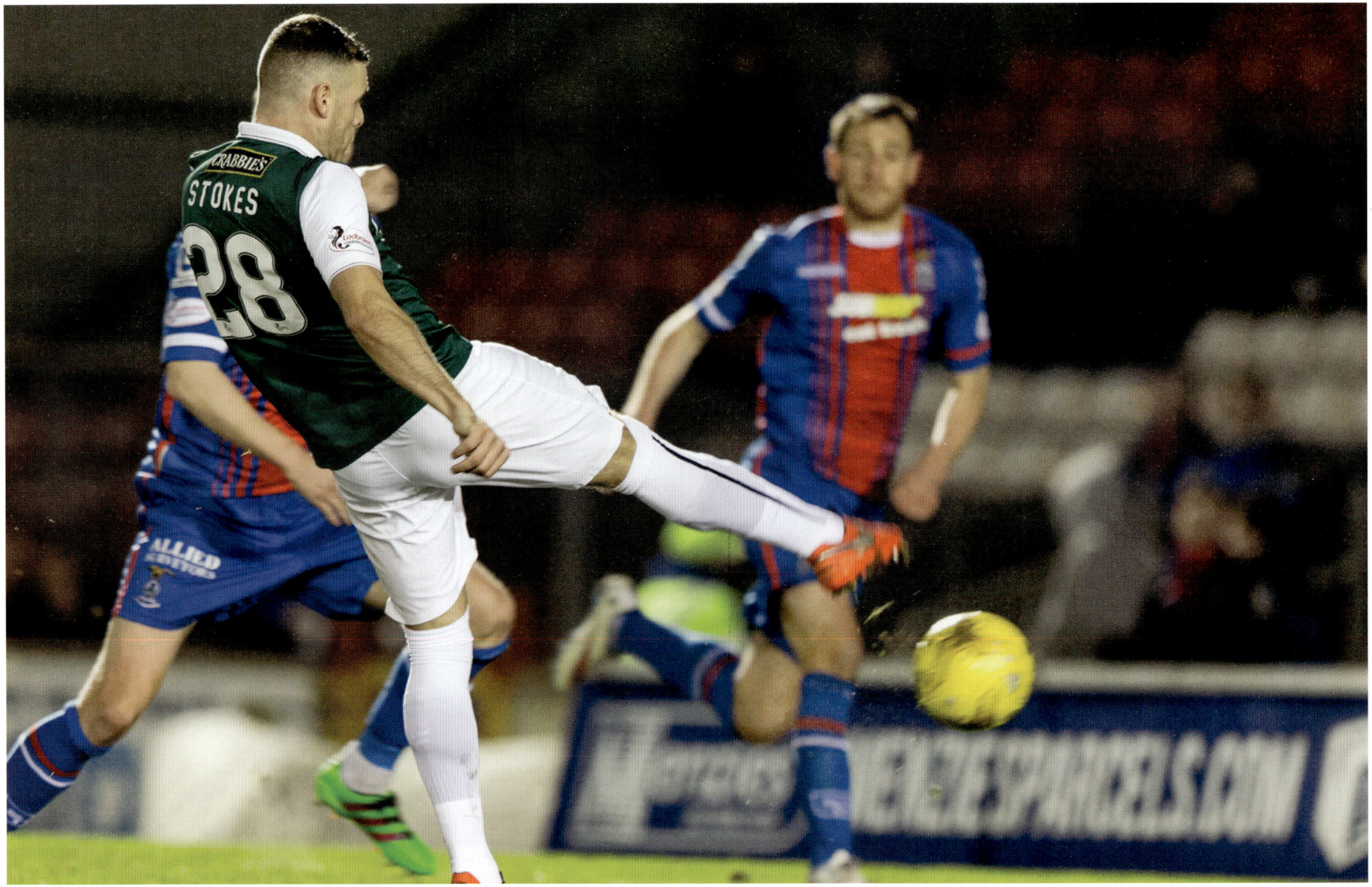
STOKES
28

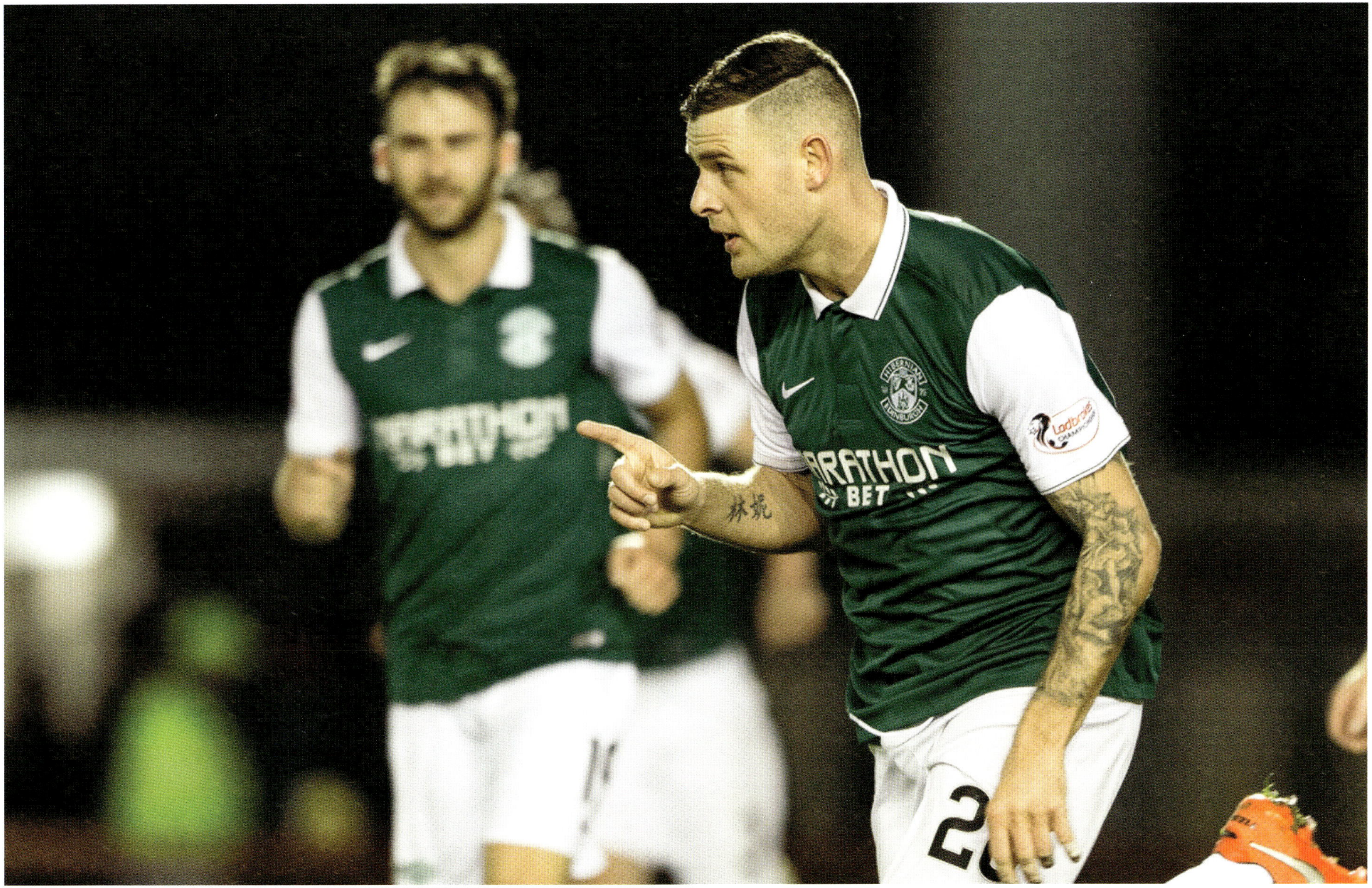

26 | A MOMENT IN TIME

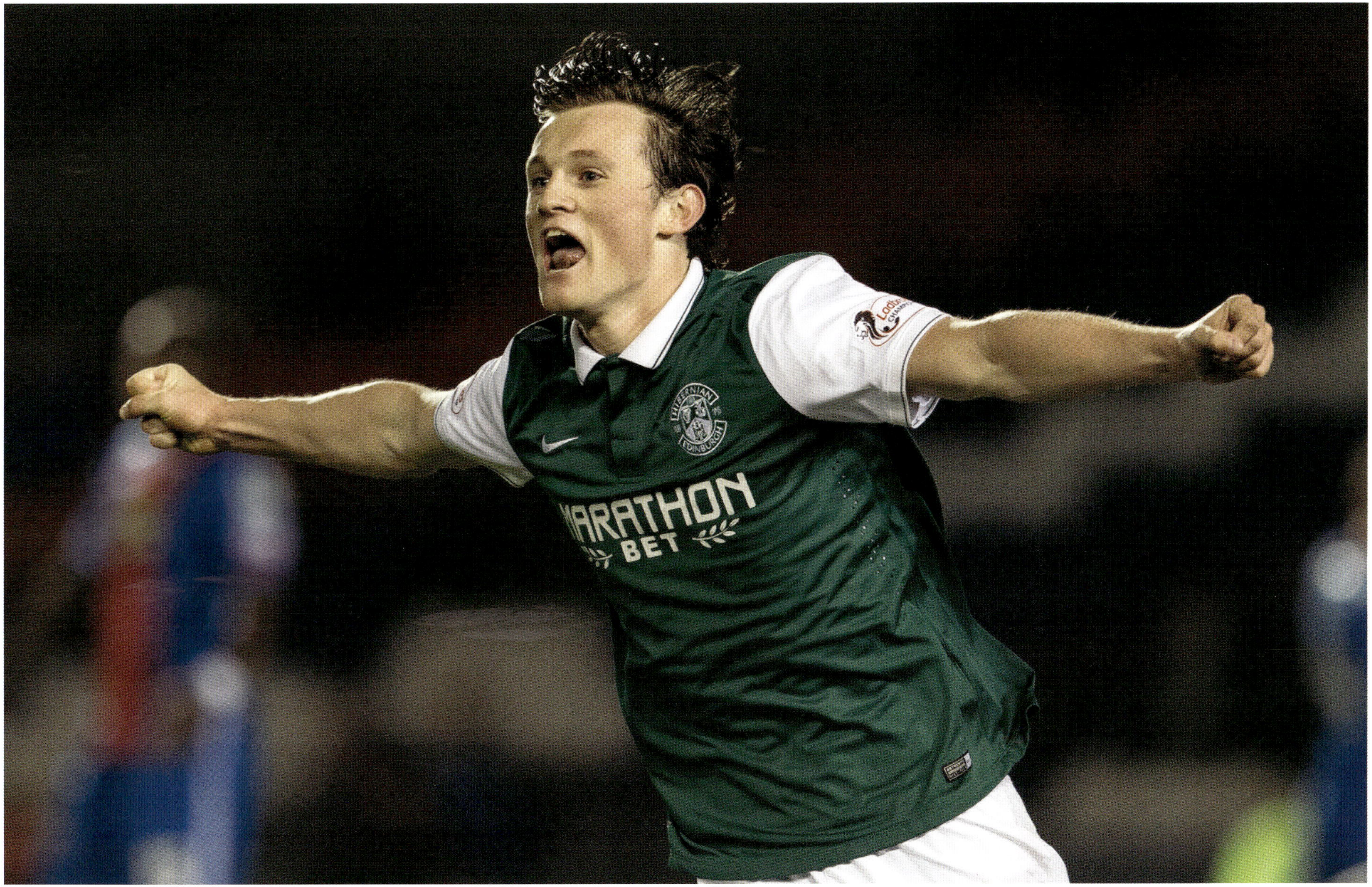
MARATHON
BET

William Hill Scottish Cup Sixth Round Replay: Inverness Caledonian Thistle 1-2 Hibernian; I. Vigurs; A. Stokes (2)

THE SEMI FINAL

"I had quite a good record penalty-wise at other clubs and had saved my fair share. After the way the day had gone, I just backed myself."

CONRAD LOGAN

30 | A MOMENT IN TIME

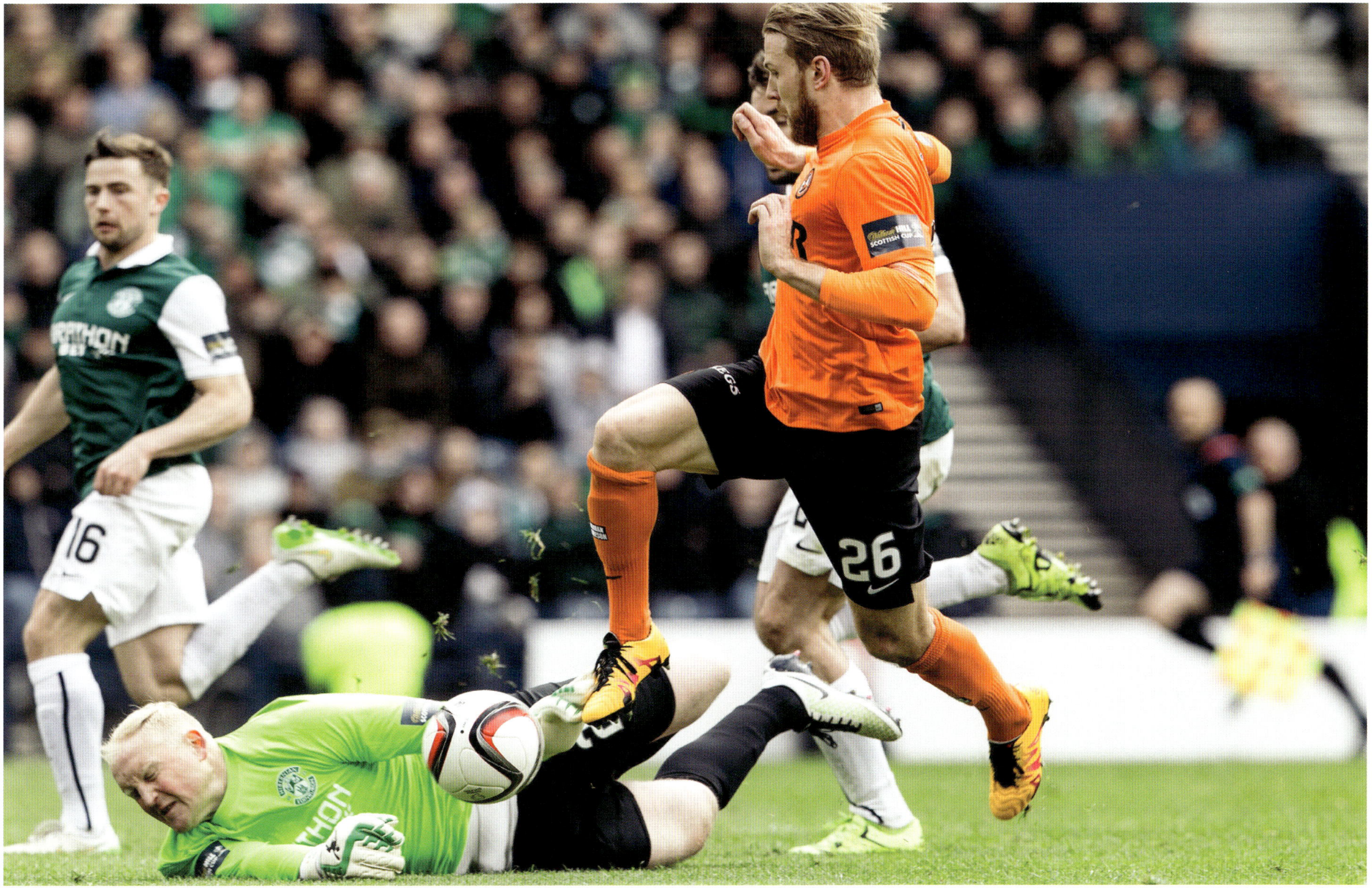
16
26
SCOTTISH CUP

32 | A MOMENT IN TIME

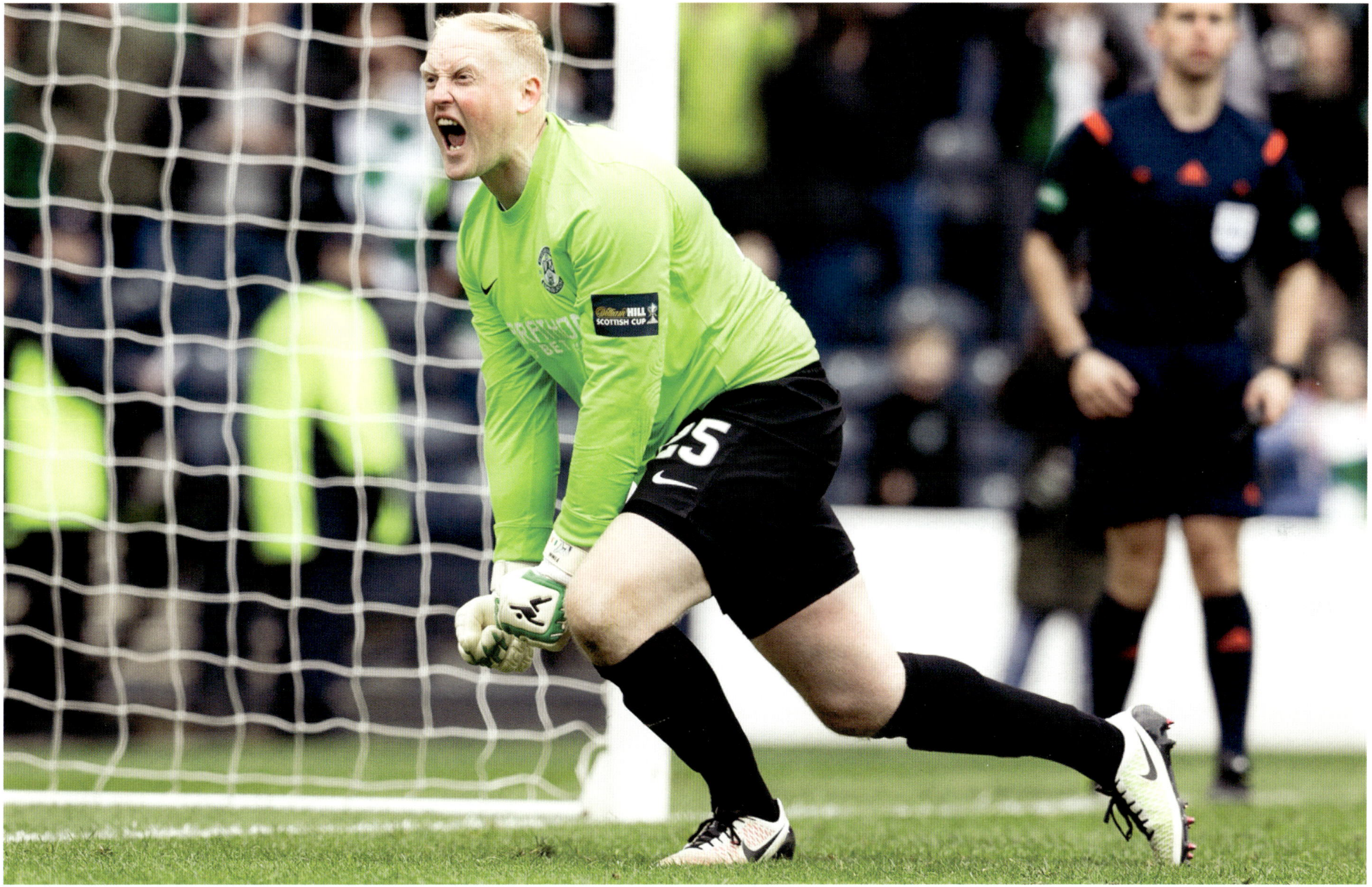
William HILL
SCOTTISH CUP
25

34 | A MOMENT IN TIME

A MOMENT IN TIME | 35

36 | A MOMENT IN TIME

A MOMENT IN TIME | 37

38 | A MOMENT IN TIME

William Hill Scottish Cup Semi Final Hibernian 0-0 Dundee United – Hibernian win 4-2 on penalties

THE FINAL

"I share a room with Liam Fontaine and we were genuinely talking about imagining scoring the winner. He said, "It'd be great to score in the 90th minute" and I went, "It needs to be later than that.""

DAVID GRAY

A MOMENT IN TIME | 41

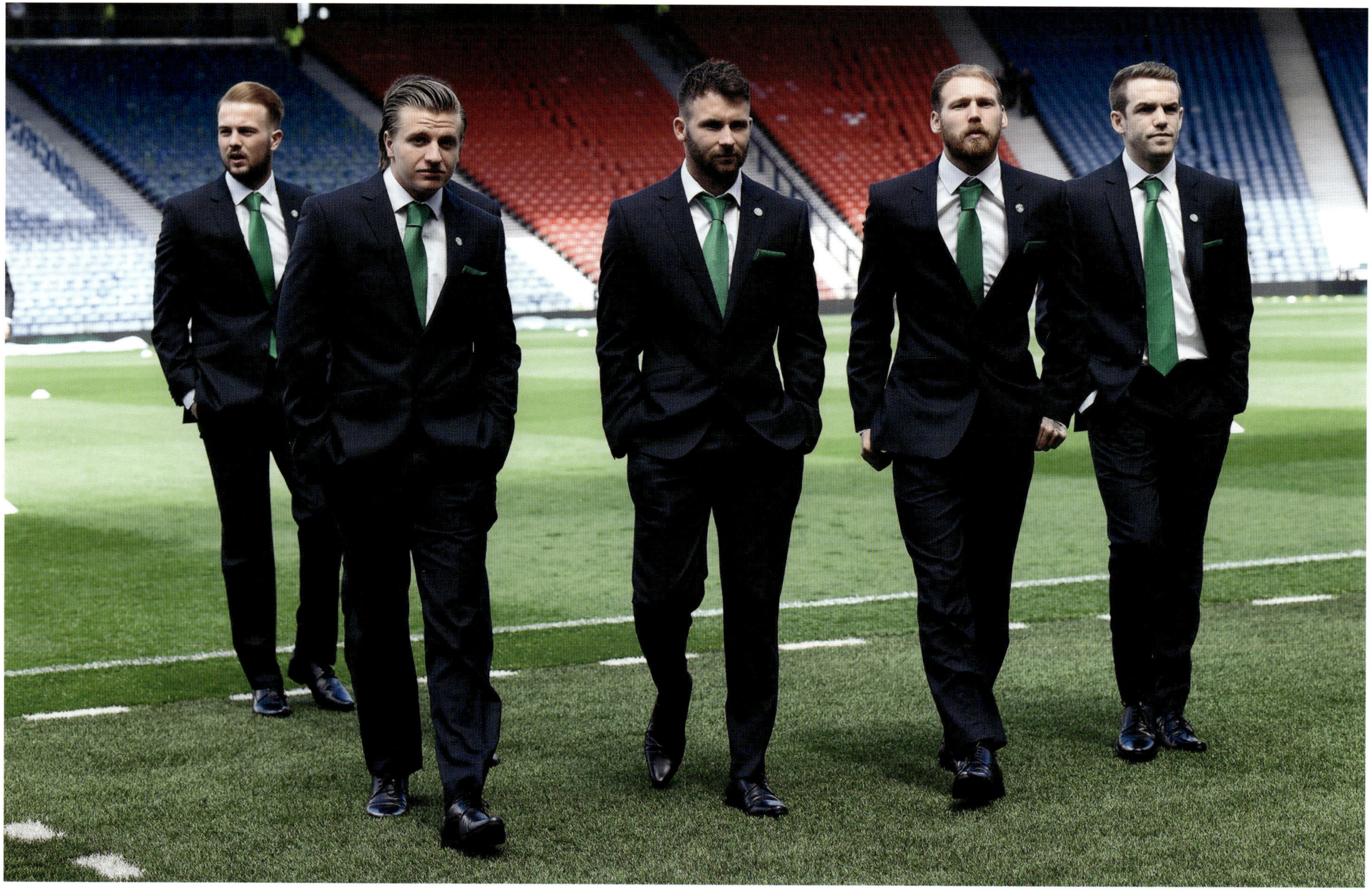

A MOMENT IN TIME | 43

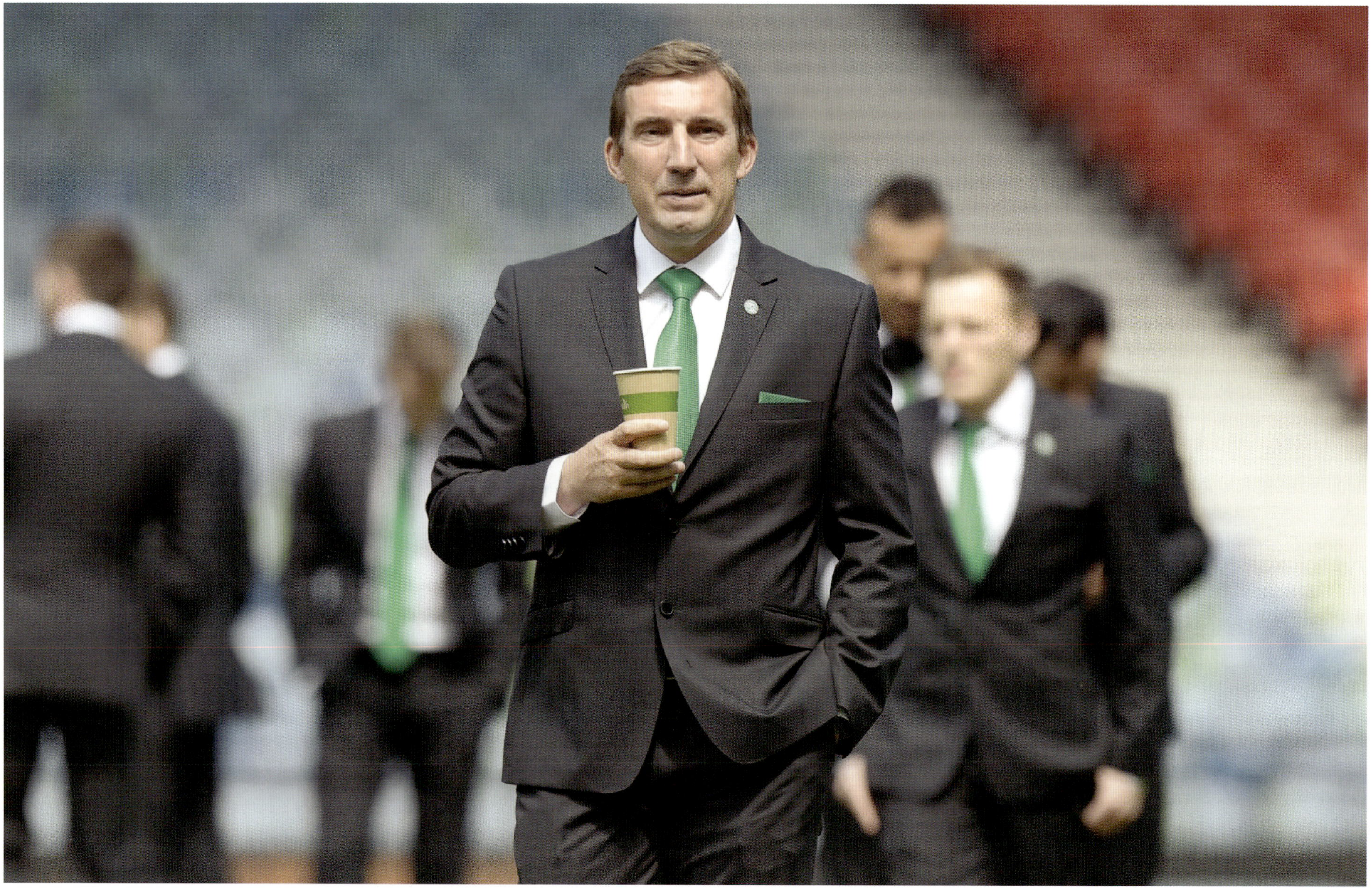

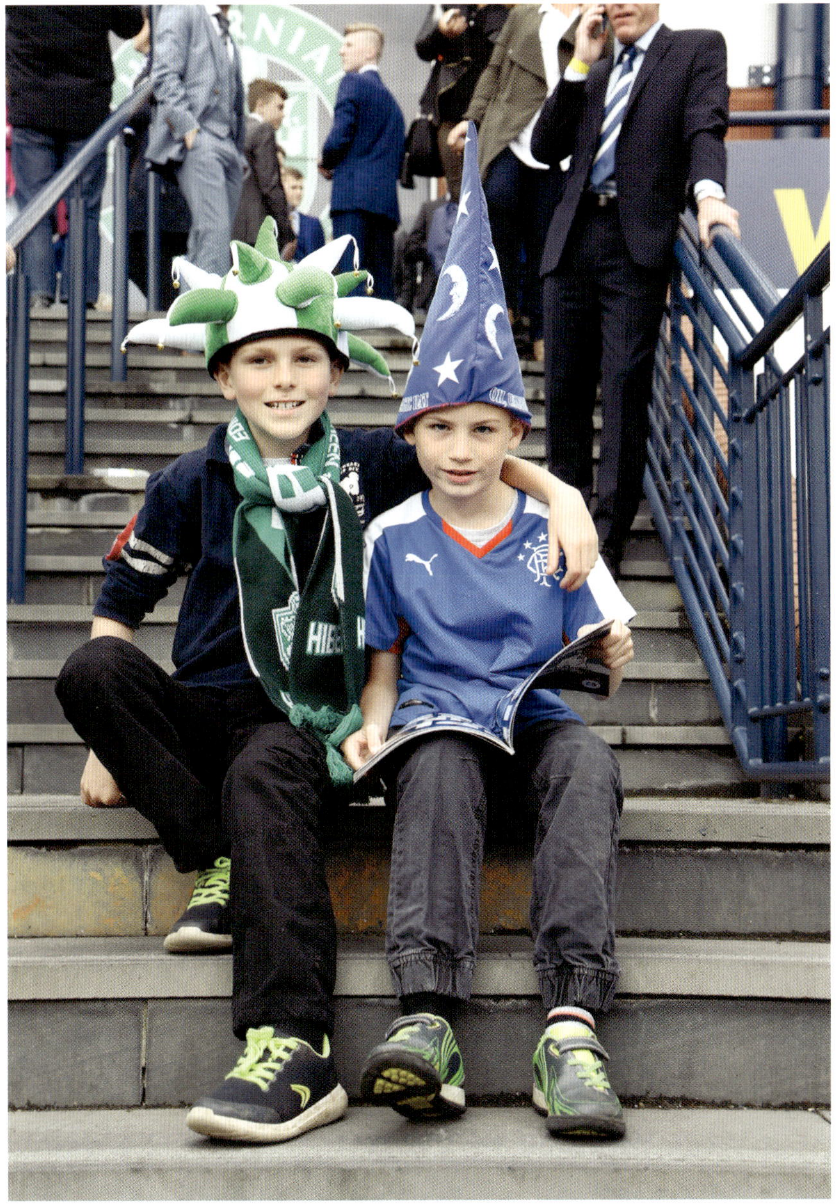

46 | A MOMENT IN TIME

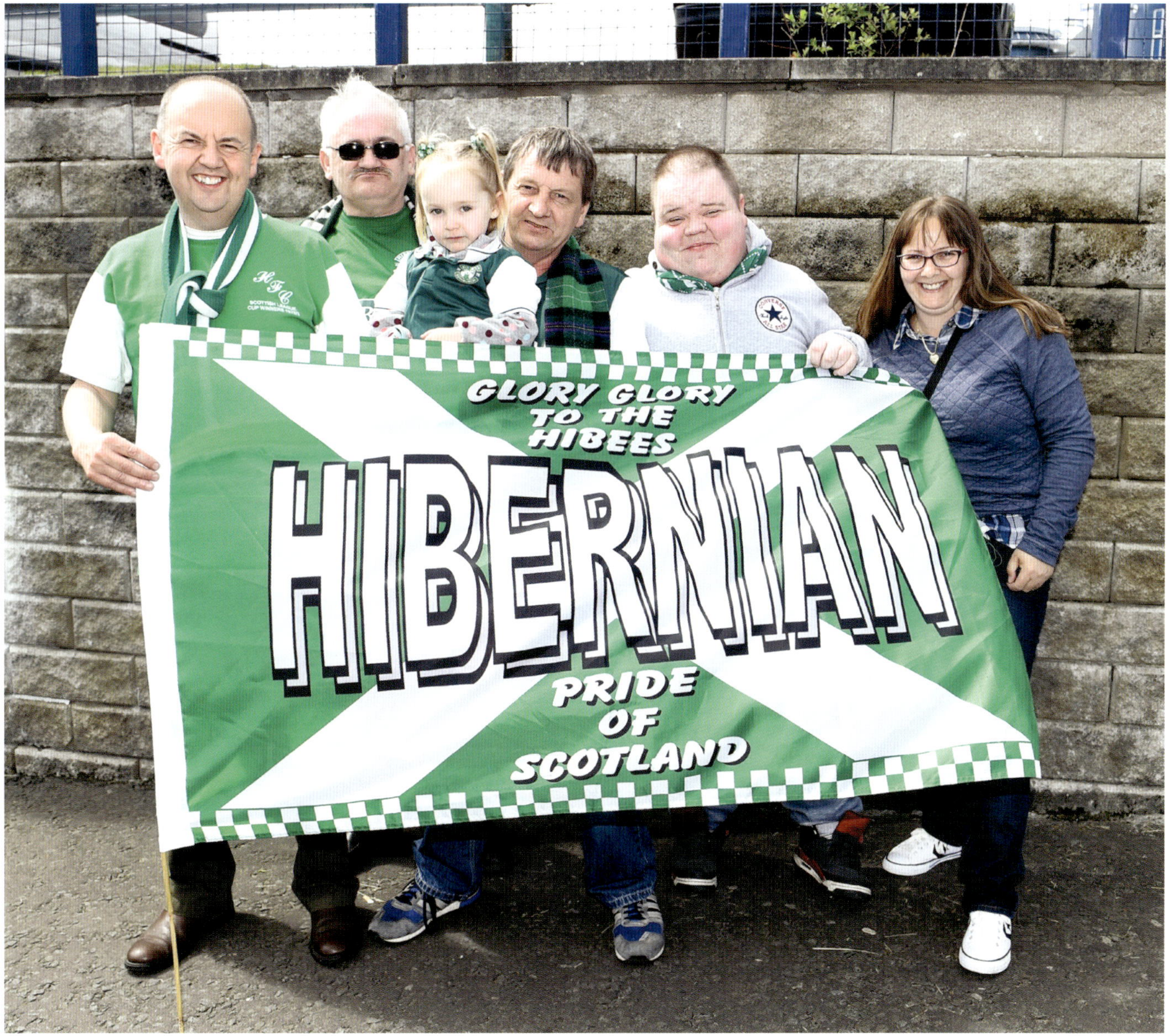
GLORY GLORY
TO THE
HIBEES
HIBERNIAN
PRIDE
OF
SCOTLAND

48 | A MOMENT IN TIME

A MOMENT IN TIME | 49

50 | A MOMENT IN TIME

A MOMENT IN TIME | 51

52 | A MOMENT IN TIME

A MOMENT IN TIME | 53

54 | A MOMENT IN TIME

A MOMENT IN TIME | 55

56 | A MOMENT IN TIME

A MOMENT IN TIME | 57

58 | A MOMENT IN TIME

A MOMENT IN TIME | 59

60 | A MOMENT IN TIME

A MOMENT IN TIME | 61

62 | A MOMENT IN TIME

A MOMENT IN TIME | 63

64 | A MOMENT IN TIME

A MOMENT IN TIME | 65

66 | A MOMENT IN TIME

A MOMENT IN TIME | 67

68 | A MOMENT IN TIME

A MOMENT IN TIME | 69

70 | A MOMENT IN TIME

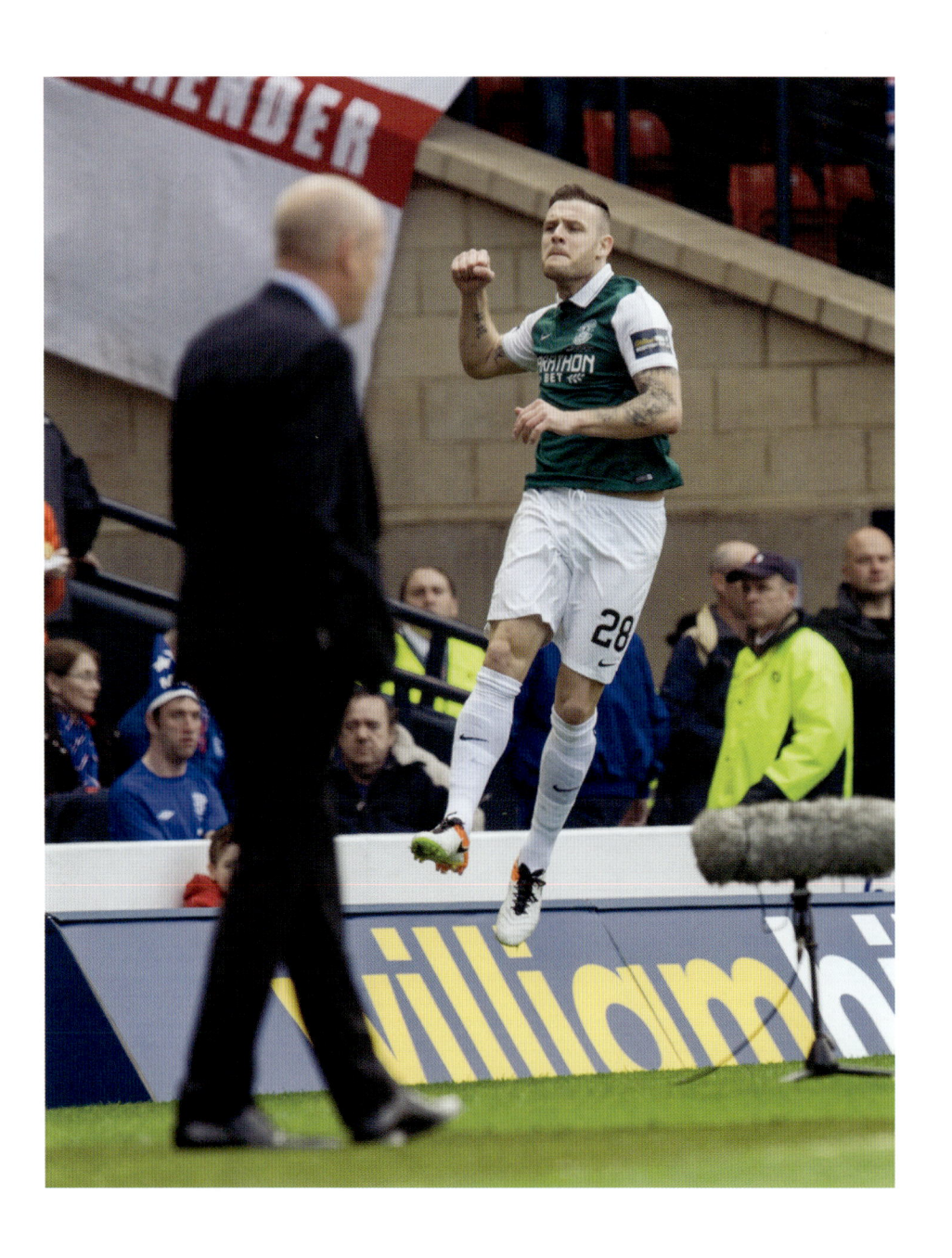

A MOMENT IN TIME | 71

72 | A MOMENT IN TIME

A MOMENT IN TIME | 73

74 | A MOMENT IN TIME

A MOMENT IN TIME | 75

76 | A MOMENT IN TIME

A MOMENT IN TIME | 77

78 | A MOMENT IN TIME

A MOMENT IN TIME | 79

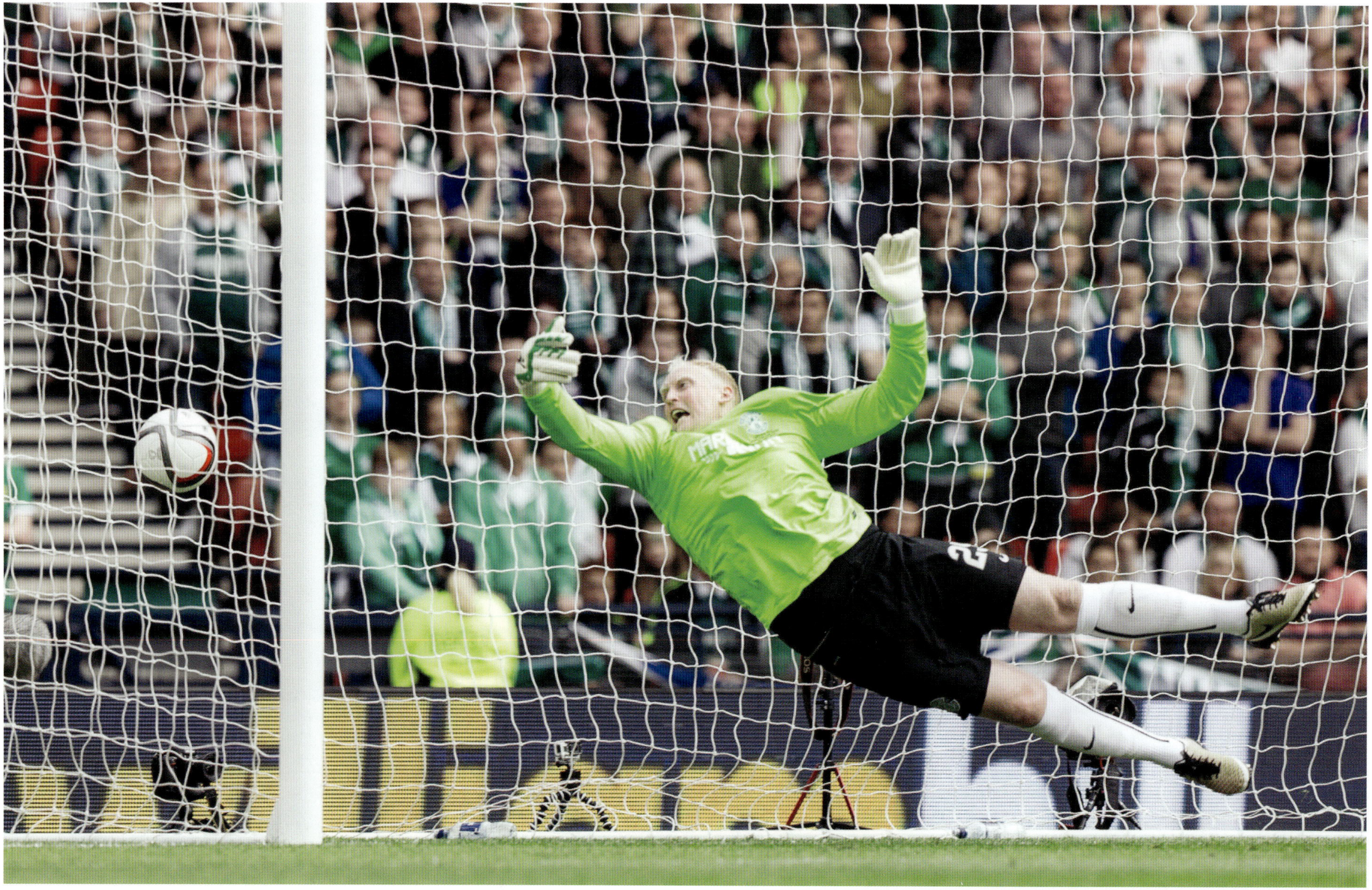

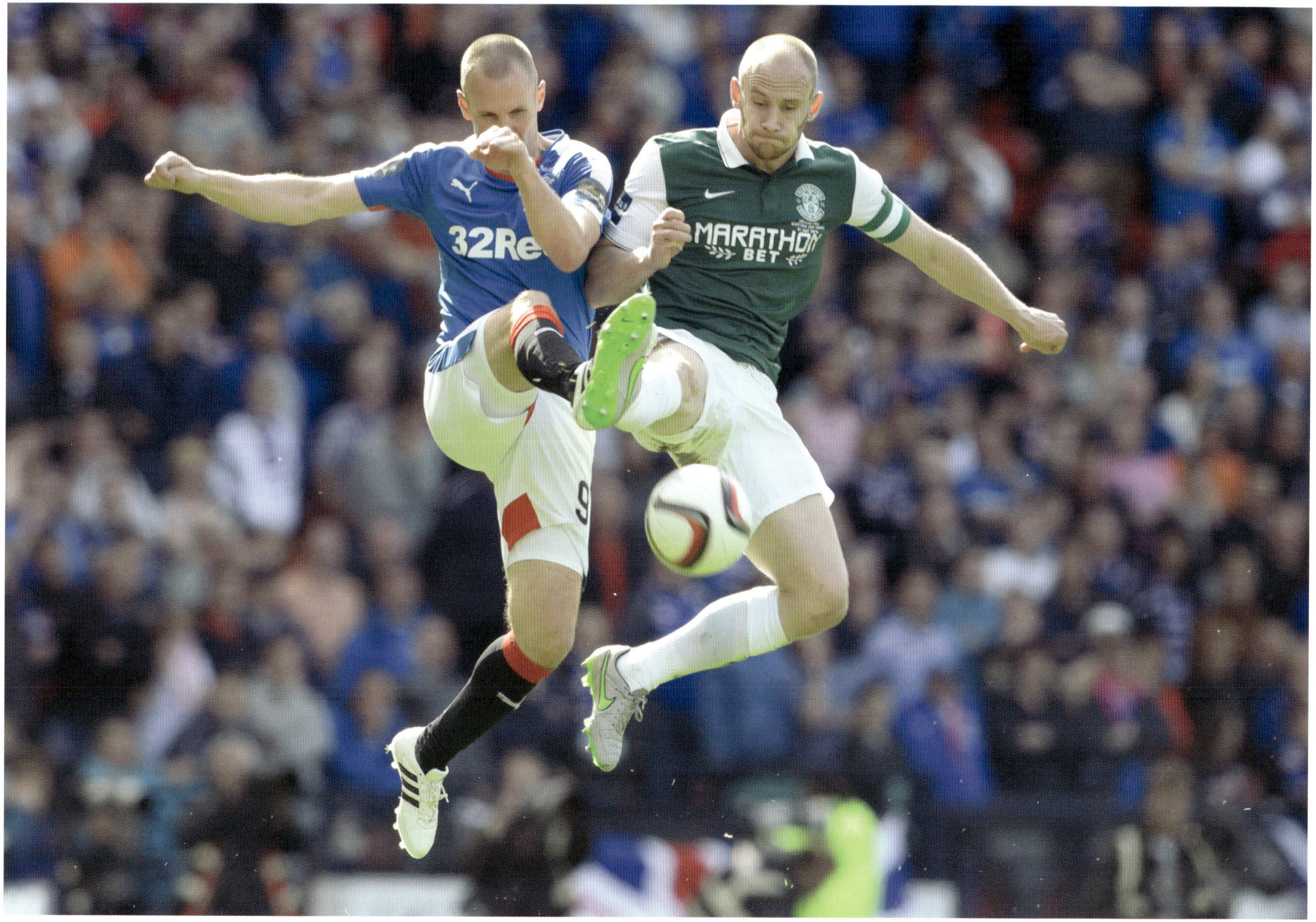
32Red
MARATHON BET

82 | A MOMENT IN TIME

A MOMENT IN TIME | 83

84 | A MOMENT IN TIME

A MOMENT IN TIME | 85

86 | A MOMENT IN TIME

A MOMENT IN TIME | 87

88 | A MOMENT IN TIME

A MOMENT IN TIME | 89

90 | A MOMENT IN TIME

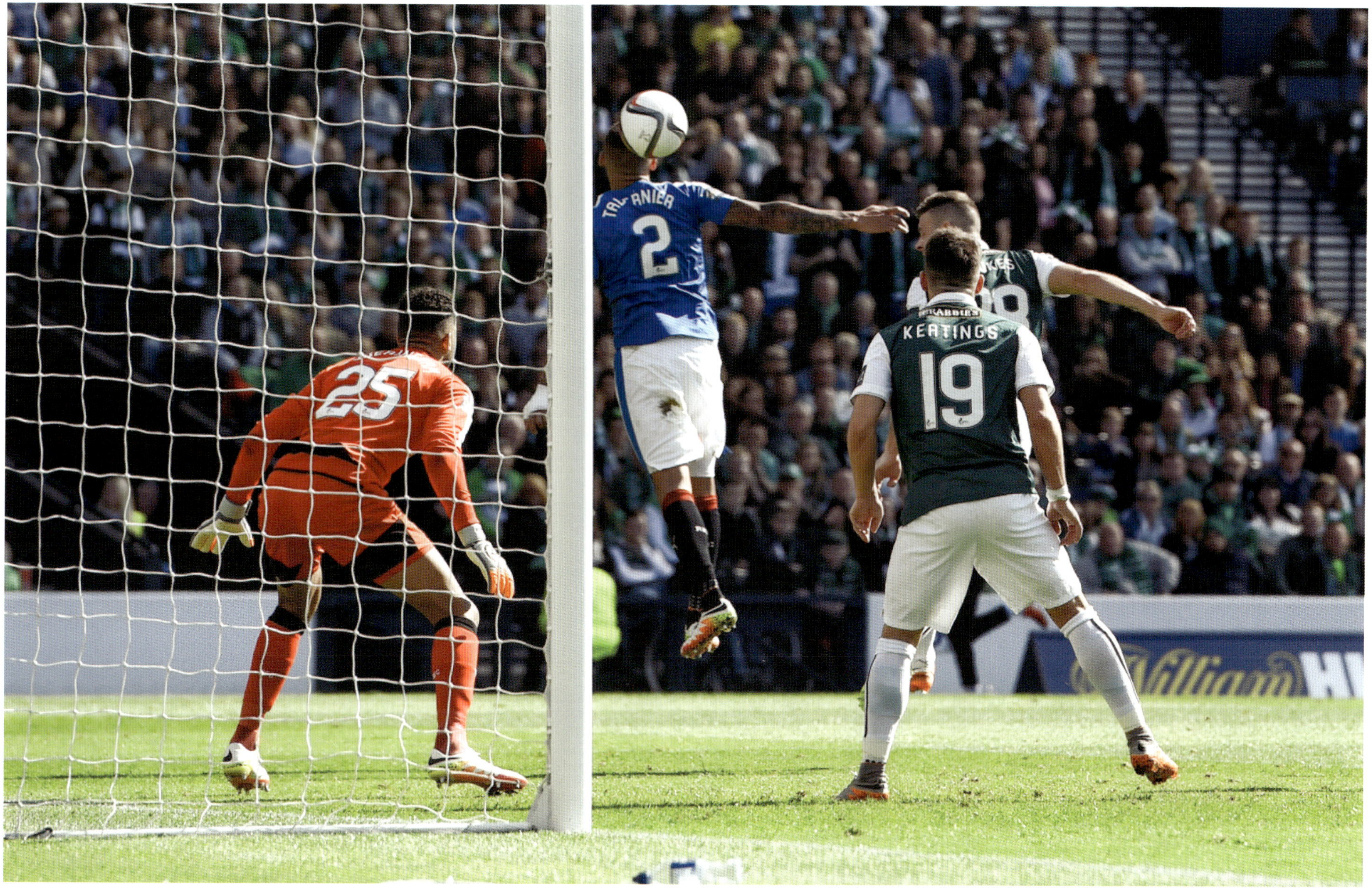
2
25
KEATINGS
19

92 | A MOMENT IN TIME

A MOMENT IN TIME | 93

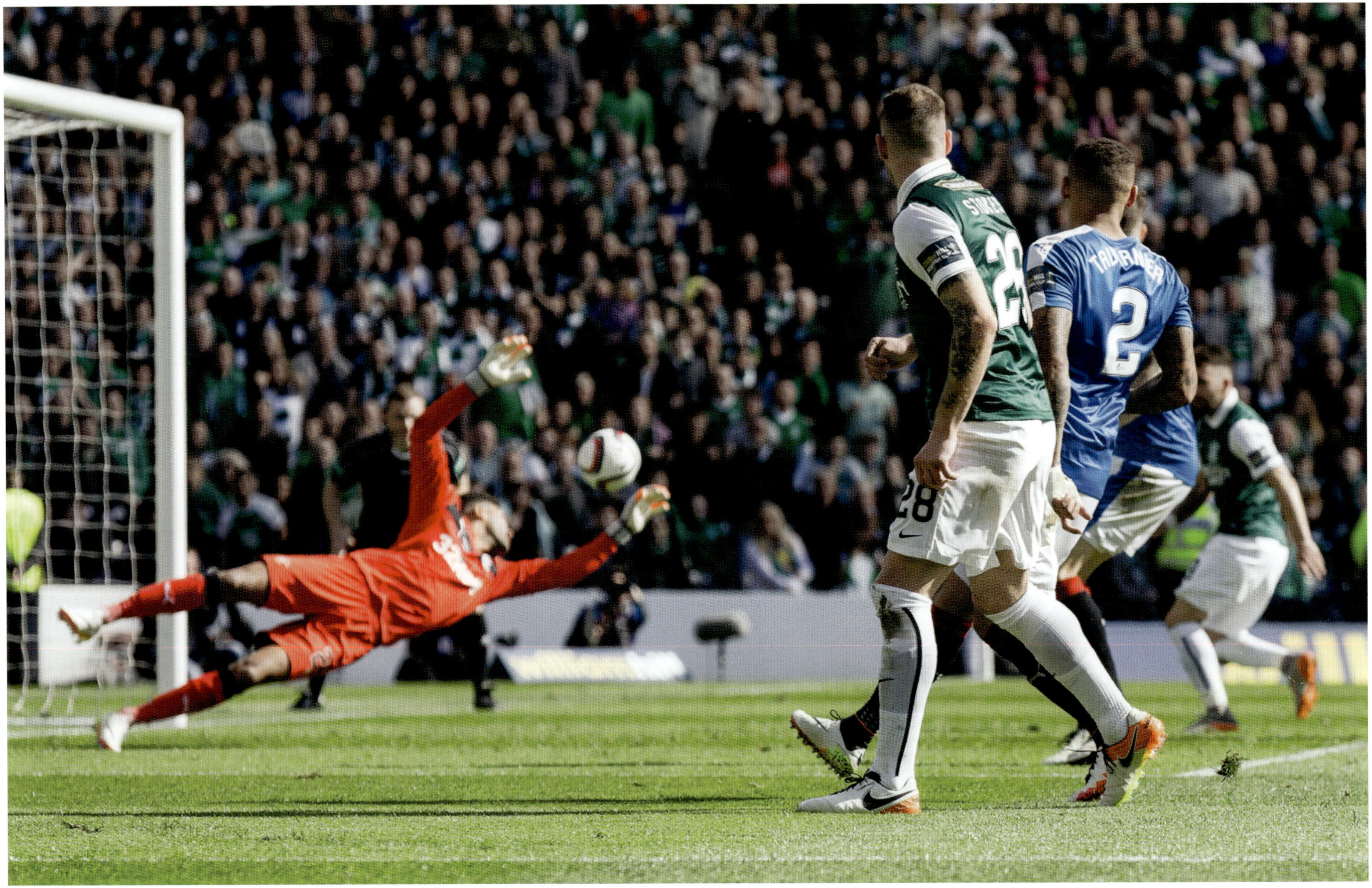

A MOMENT IN TIME | 95

96 | A MOMENT IN TIME

A MOMENT IN TIME | 97

98 | A MOMENT IN TIME

A MOMENT IN TIME | 99

100 | A MOMENT IN TIME

A MOMENT IN TIME | 101

102 | A MOMENT IN TIME

A MOMENT IN TIME | 103

104 | A MOMENT IN TIME

A MOMENT IN TIME | 105

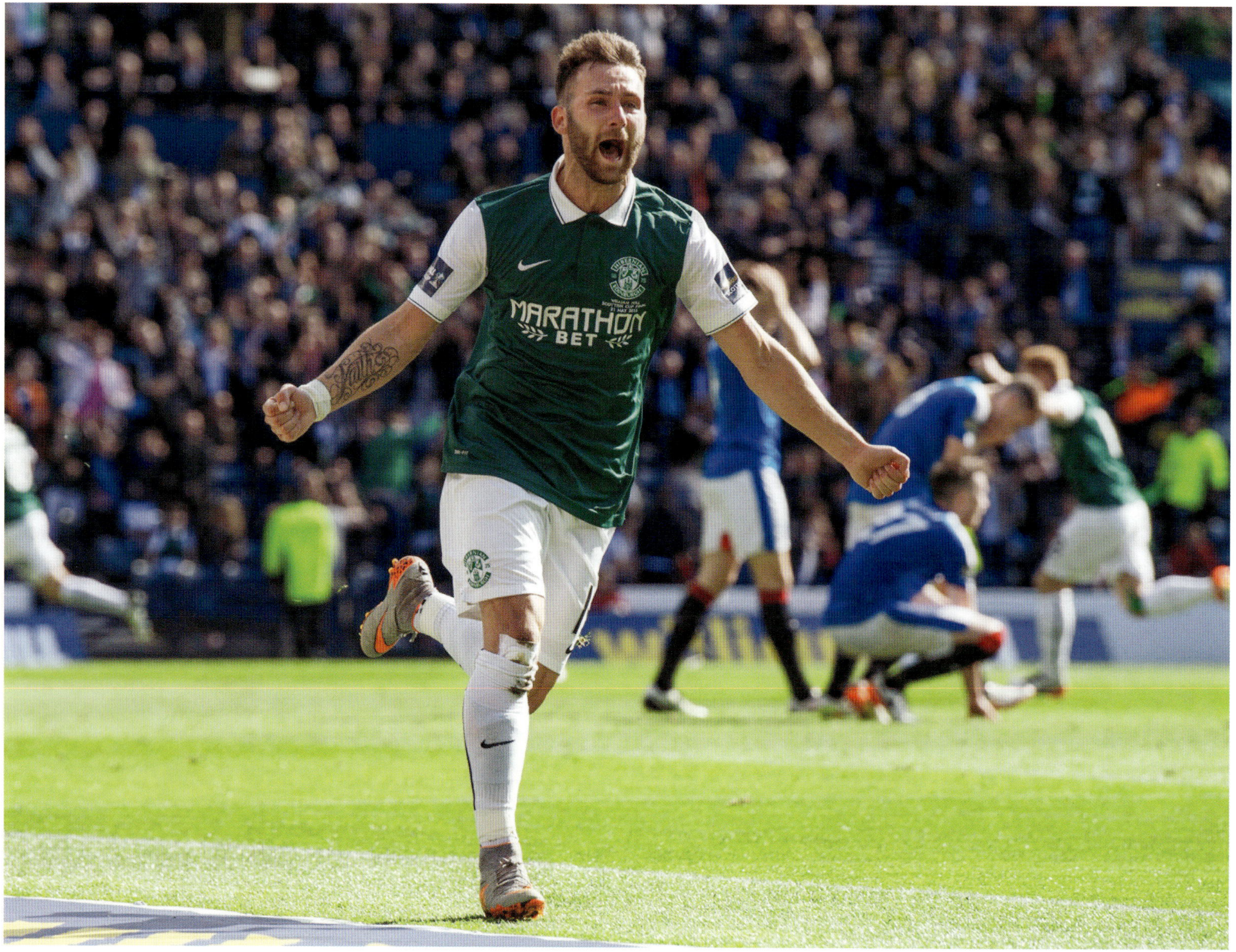
MARATHON
BET

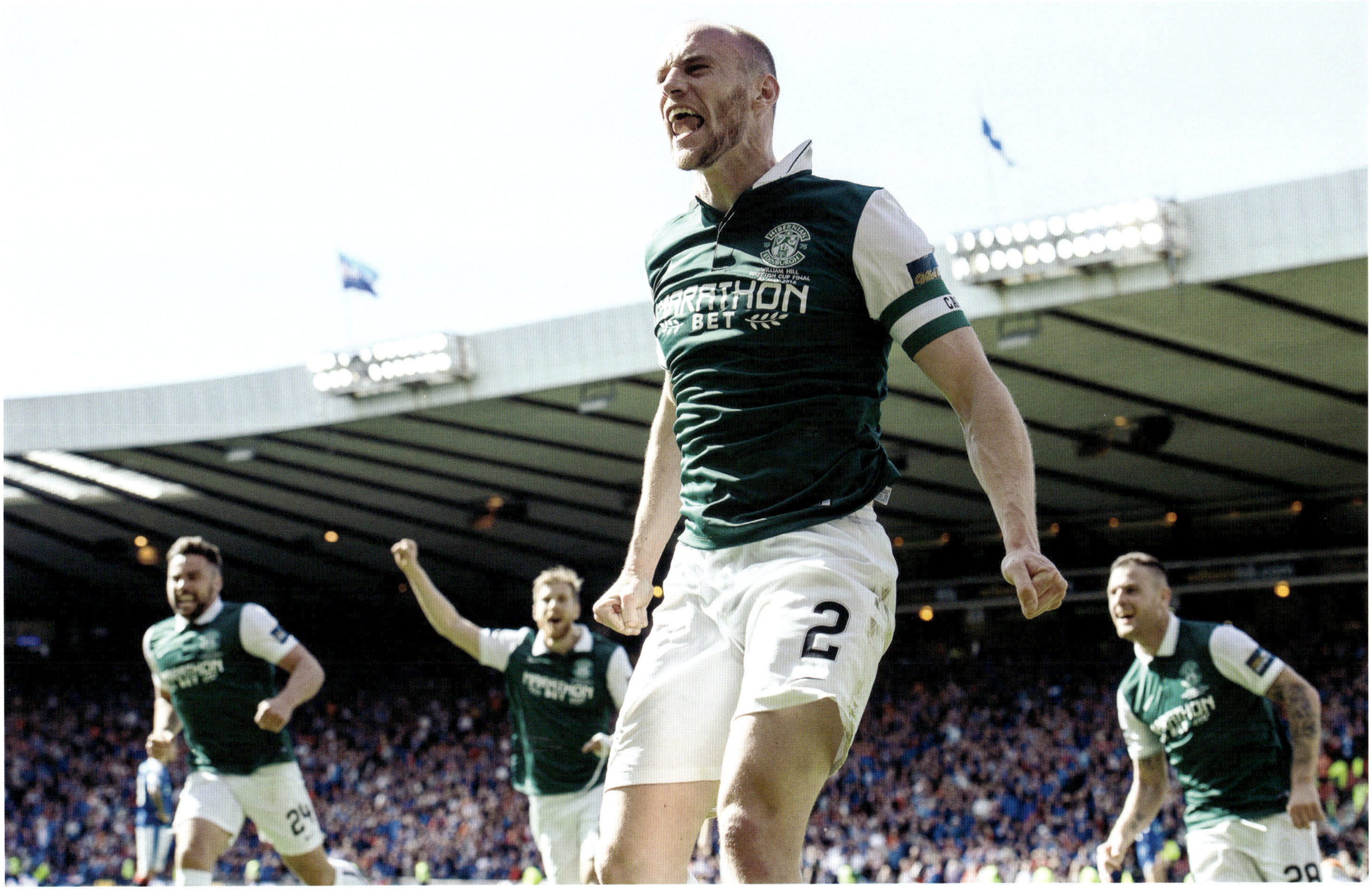
BET
2

108 | A MOMENT IN TIME

A MOMENT IN TIME | 109

110 | A MOMENT IN TIME

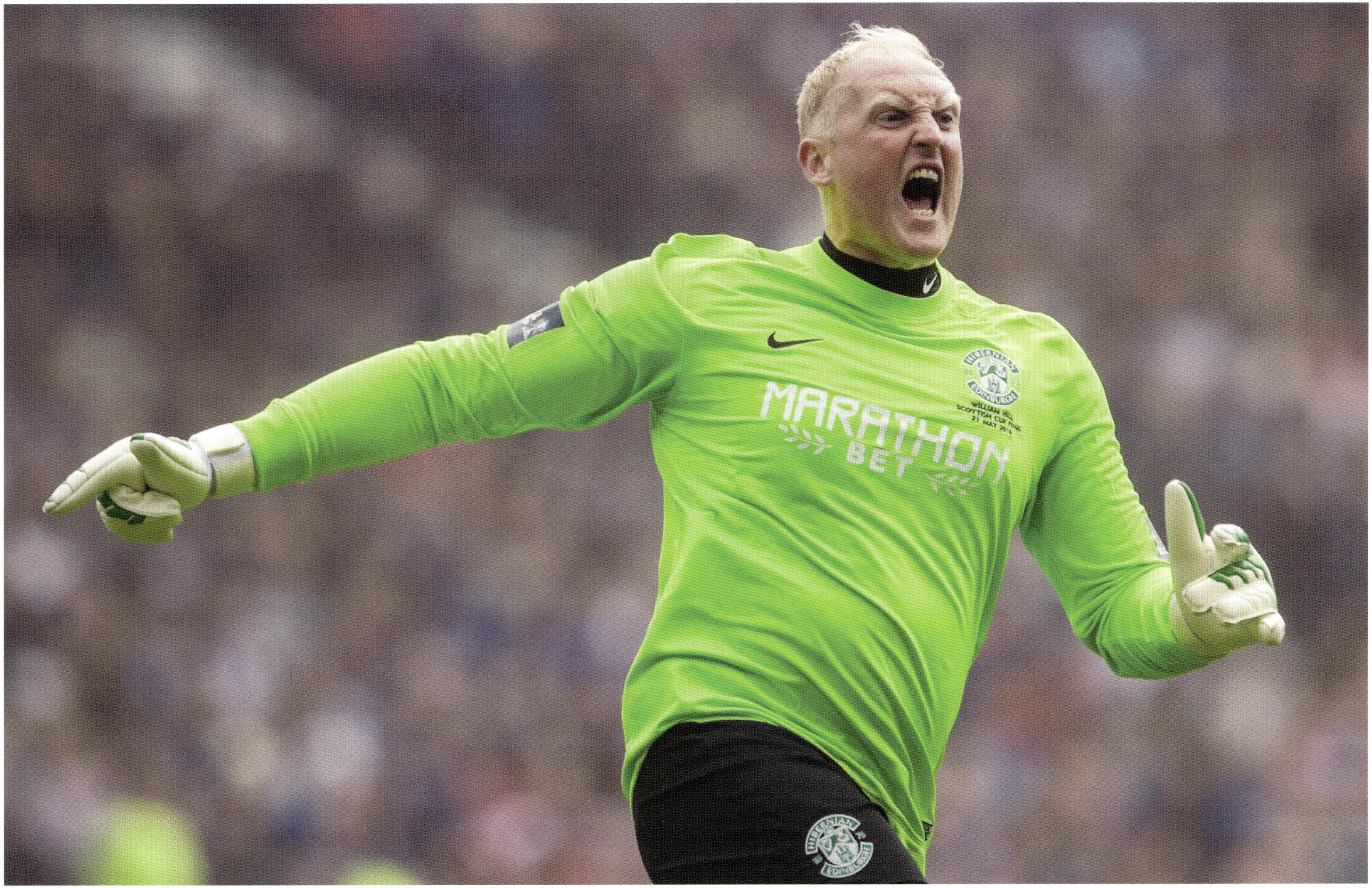
MARATHON
BET

112 | A MOMENT IN TIME

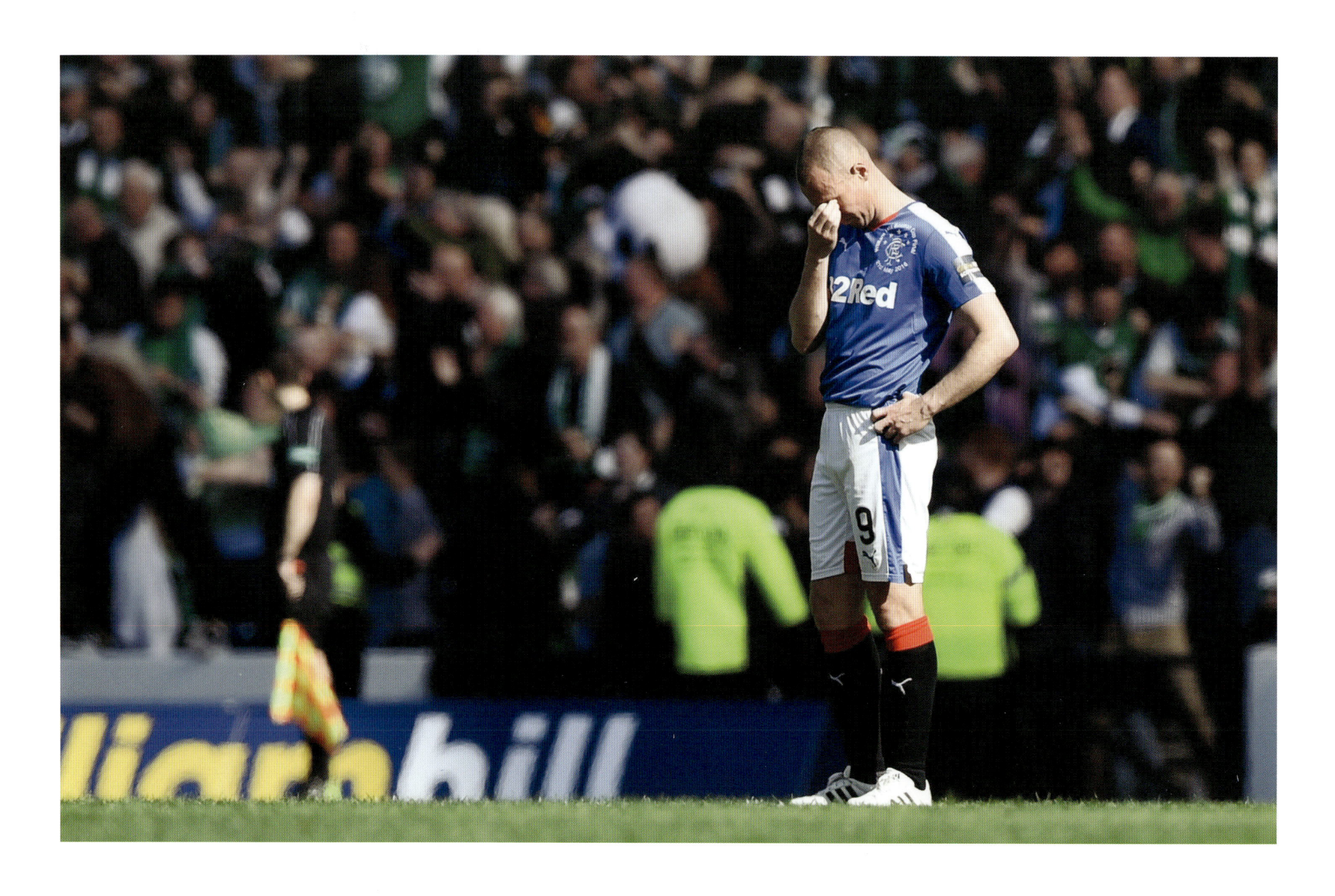

A MOMENT IN TIME | 113

114 | A MOMENT IN TIME

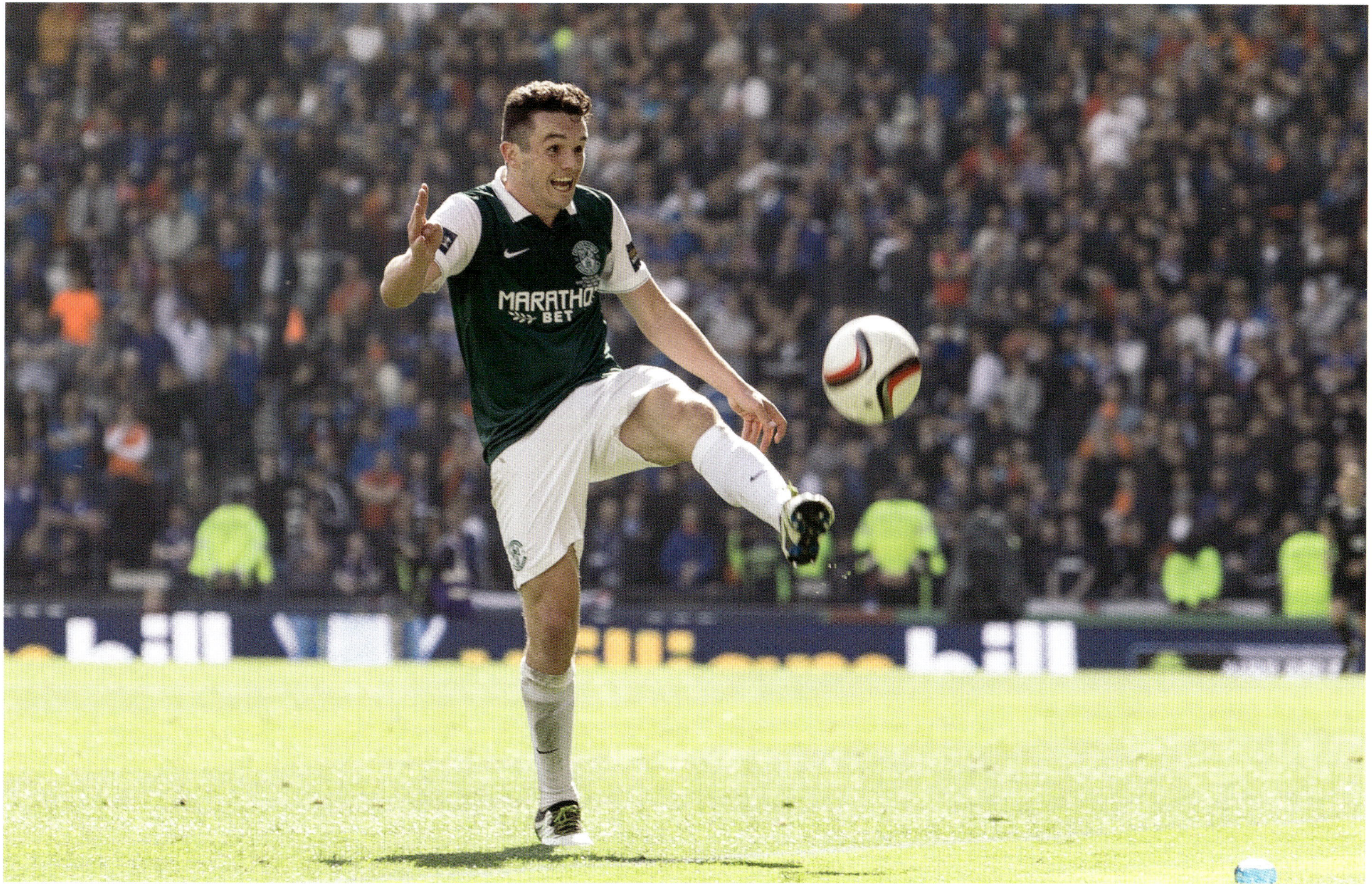
MARATHON
BET

116 | A MOMENT IN TIME

William Hill Scottish Cup Final: Rangers 2-3 Hibernian; K. Miller, A. Halliday; A. Stokes (2), D. Gray

118 | A MOMENT IN TIME

A MOMENT IN TIME | 119

PRIDE OF EASTER ROAD
SCOTTISH CUP FINAL
21 MAY 2016
HIBERNIAN F.C.
CIS CUP FINAL 2007

A MOMENT IN TIME | 121

122 | A MOMENT IN TIME

THE PRESENTATION

"Having a hand in bringing the trophy back to Leith, somewhere I was born and bred, and with a team I had always supported – it was too much for me to take in."

DARREN MCGREGOR

124 | A MOMENT IN TIME

A MOMENT IN TIME | 125

126 | A MOMENT IN TIME

A MOMENT IN TIME | 127

128 | A MOMENT IN TIME

A MOMENT IN TIME | 129

130 | A MOMENT IN TIME

A MOMENT IN TIME | 131

132 | A MOMENT IN TIME

A MOMENT IN TIME | 133

134 | A MOMENT IN TIME

A MOMENT IN TIME | 135

136 | A MOMENT IN TIME

A MOMENT IN TIME | 137

138 | A MOMENT IN TIME

A MOMENT IN TIME | 139

William Hill
WILLIAM HILL
SCOTTISH CUP FINAL
21 MAY 2016
williamhill.com

A MOMENT IN TIME | 141

142 | A MOMENT IN TIME

A MOMENT IN TIME | 143

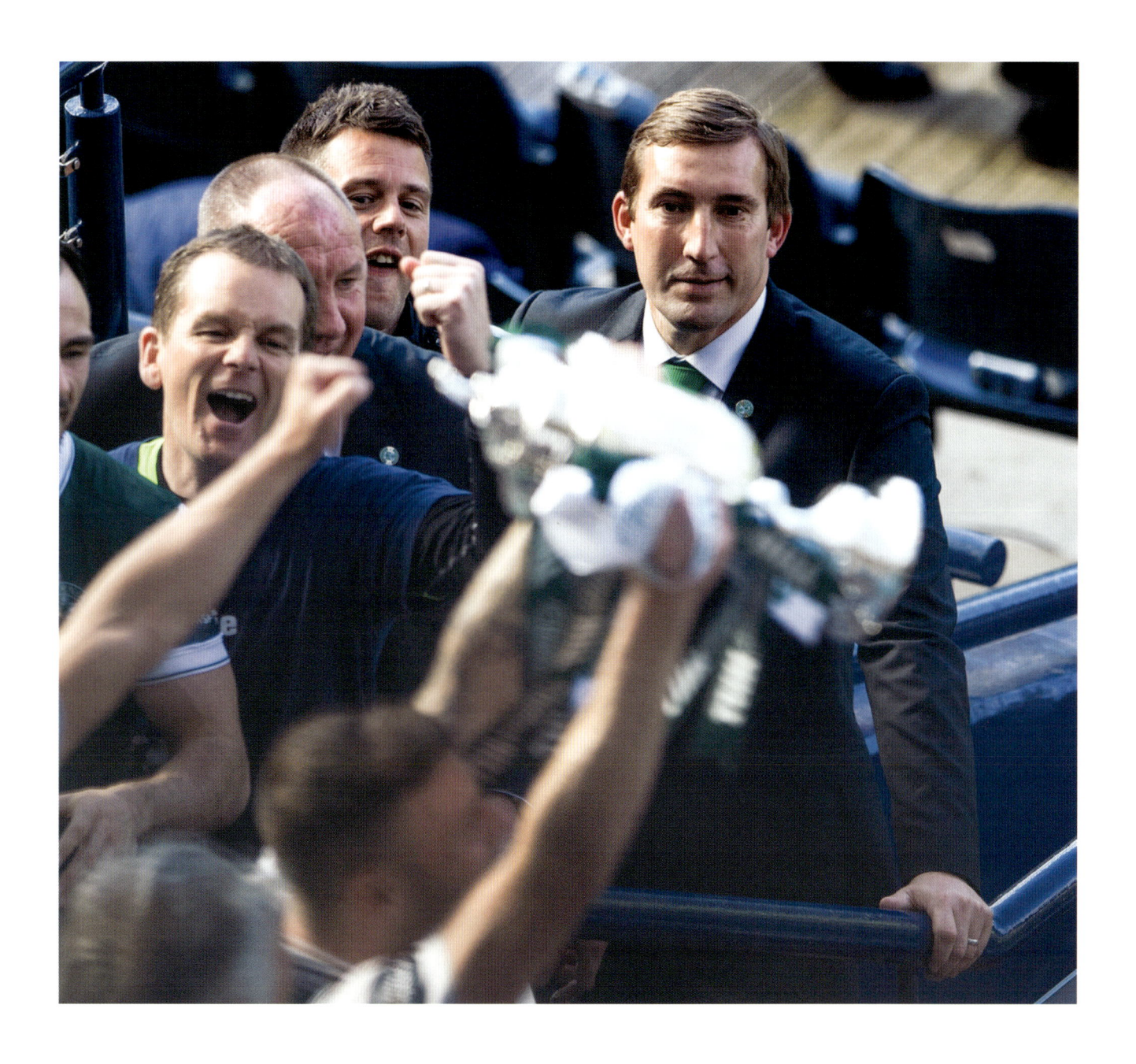

144 | A MOMENT IN TIME

A MOMENT IN TIME | 145

146 | A MOMENT IN TIME

A MOMENT IN TIME | 147

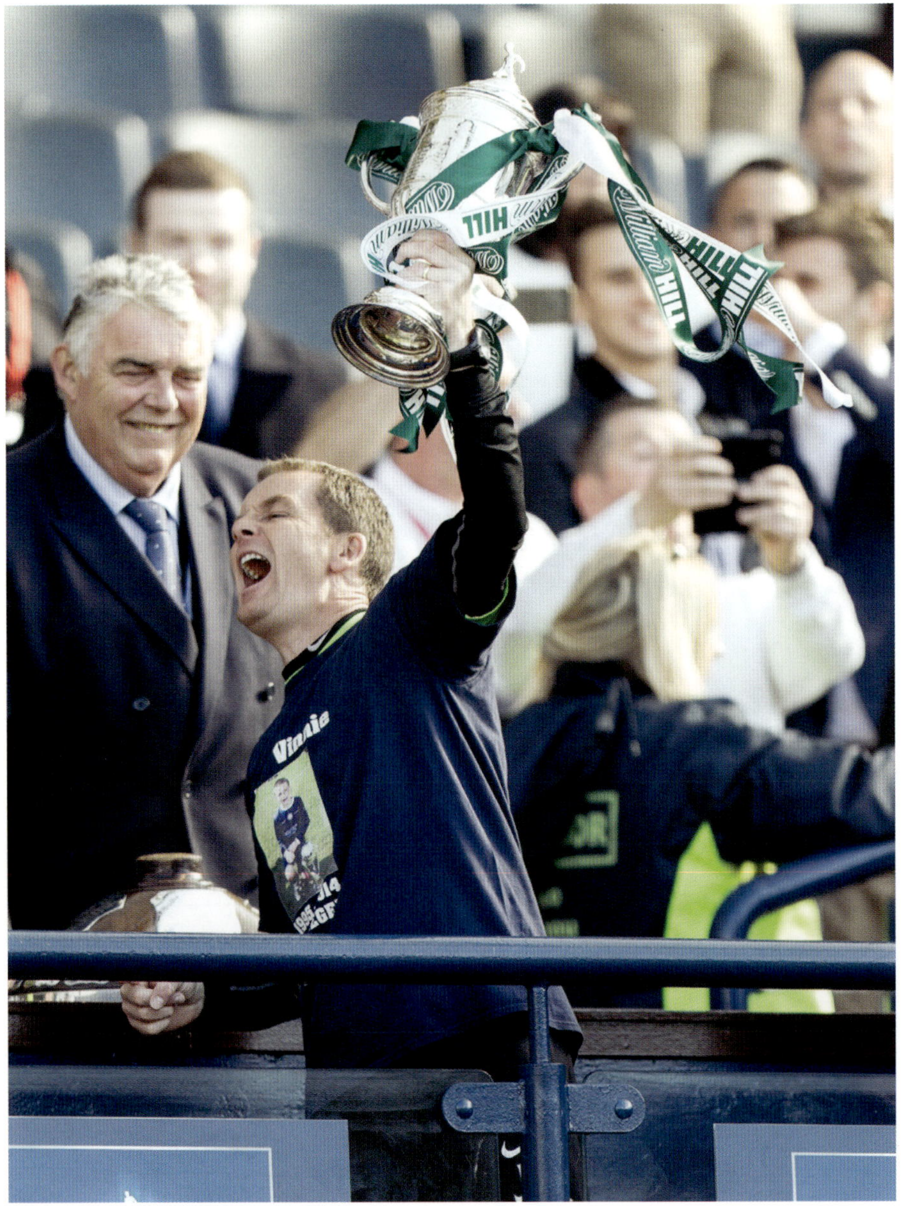

A MOMENT IN TIME | 149

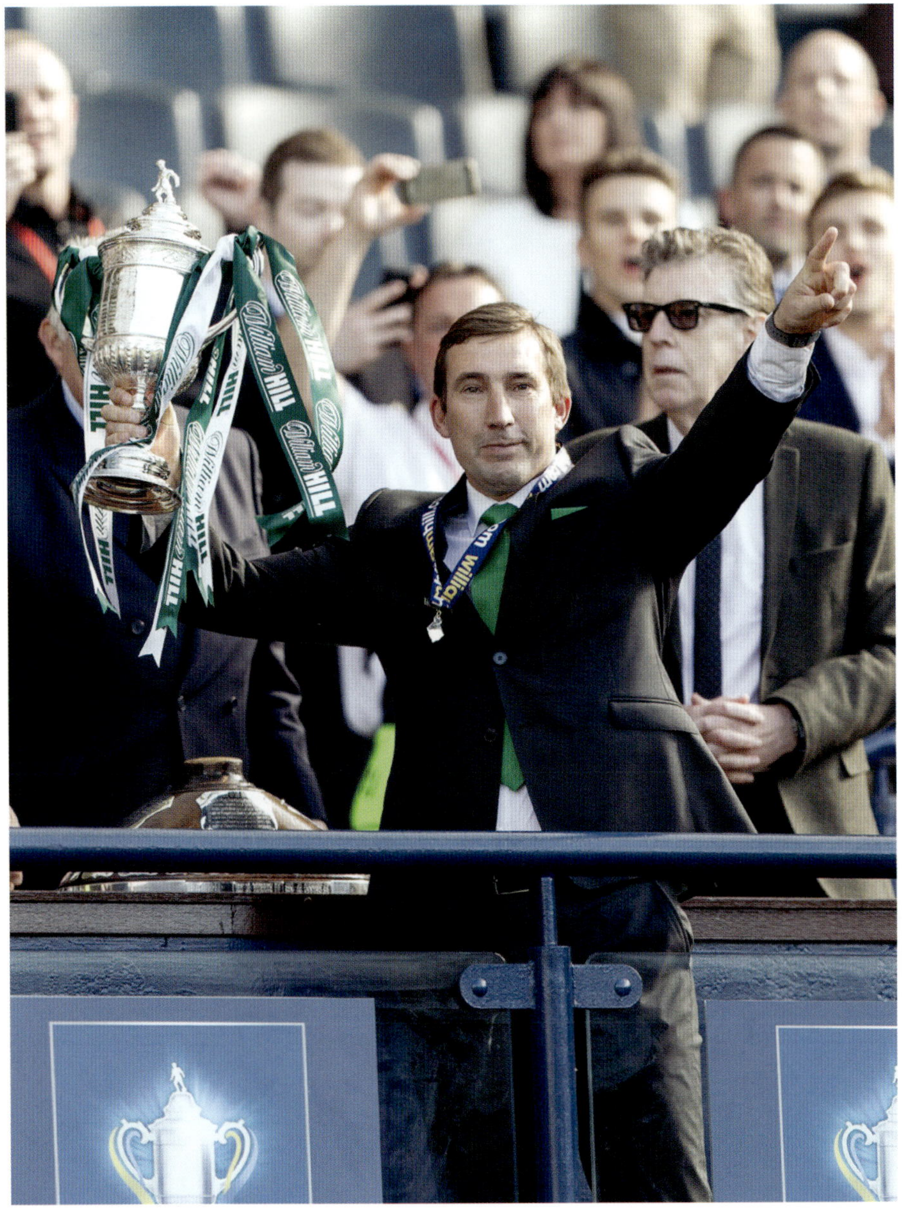
HILL

A MOMENT IN TIME | 151

152 | A MOMENT IN TIME

A MOMENT IN TIME | 153

154 | A MOMENT IN TIME

A MOMENT IN TIME | 155

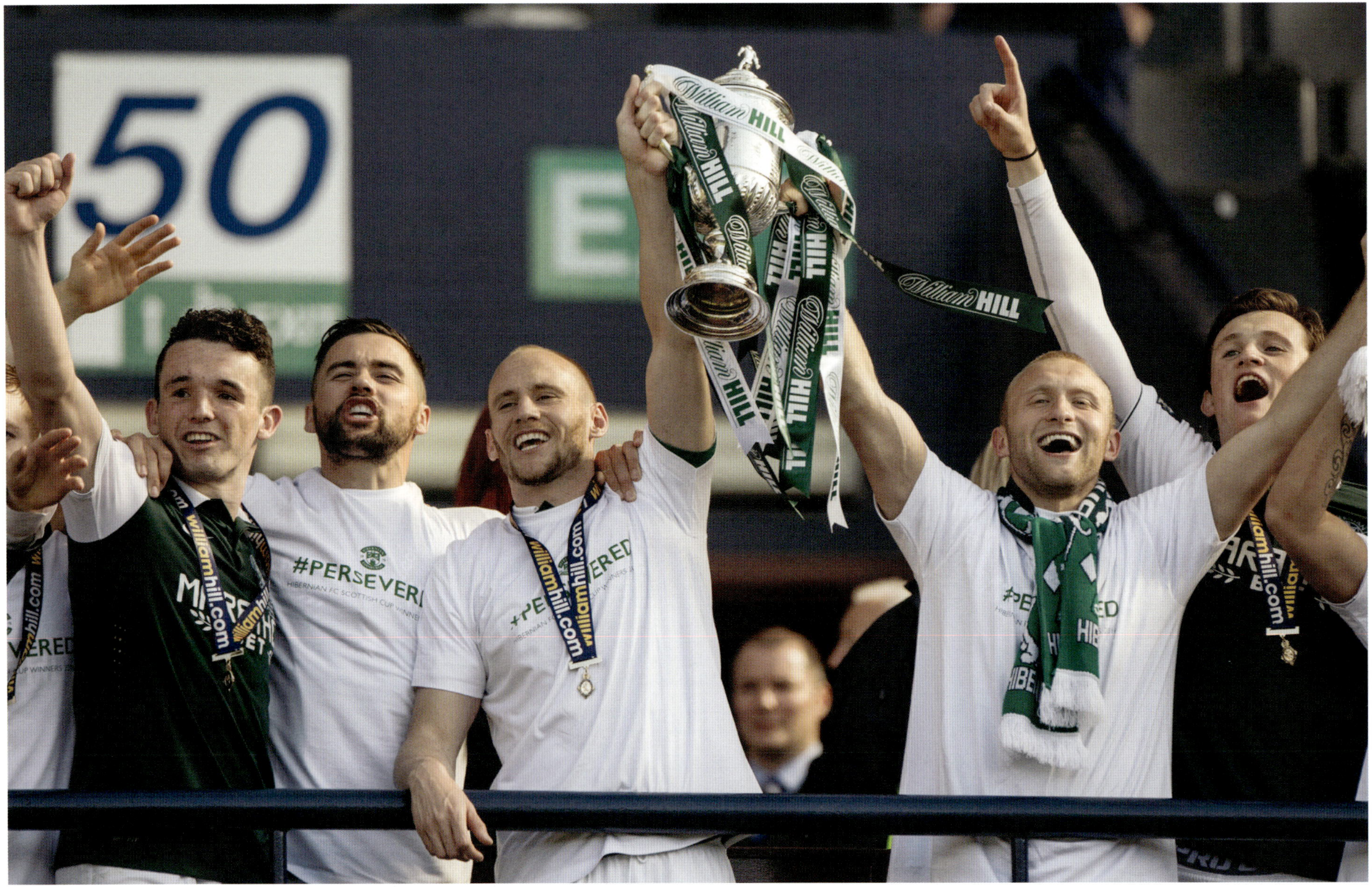
50
William HILL
williamhill.com

A MOMENT IN TIME | 157

158 | A MOMENT IN TIME

A MOMENT IN TIME | 159

160 | A MOMENT IN TIME

A MOMENT IN TIME | 161

162 | A MOMENT IN TIME

THE DRESSING ROOM

"To come back in after such a long season and the disappointment that we'd had, to win the Scottish Cup, it was just class."

LIAM FONTAINE

164 | A MOMENT IN TIME

A MOMENT IN TIME | 165

166 | A MOMENT IN TIME

A MOMENT IN TIME | 167

168 | A MOMENT IN TIME

A MOMENT IN TIME | 169

170 | A MOMENT IN TIME

A MOMENT IN TIME | 171

172 | A MOMENT IN TIME

A MOMENT IN TIME | 173

174 | A MOMENT IN TIME

THE PARADE

"The open top bus was just mind-blowing. We turned off the end of Princes Street and looked to enter Leith Walk. Everybody was stood open-mouthed. It was just absolutely mind-blowing."

ALAN STUBBS

176 | A MOMENT IN TIME

A MOMENT IN TIME | 177

178 | A MOMENT IN TIME

A MOMENT IN TIME | 179

MARATHON BET
HIBERNIAN FC
SCOTTISH CUP WINNERS 2016
534
Lothian Buses
W634 PSX
EVENT STAFF

A MOMENT IN TIME | 181

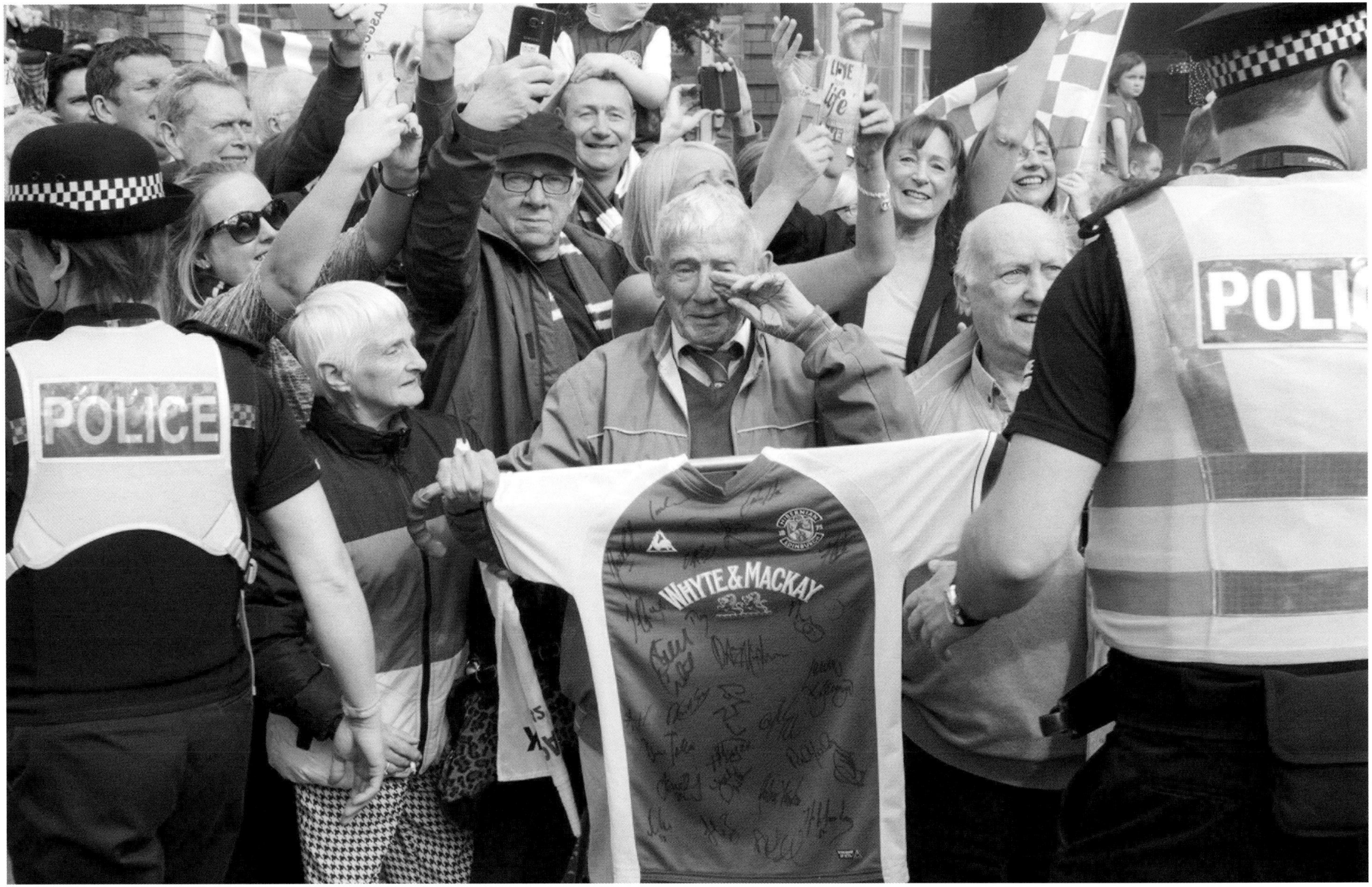
POLICE
WHYTE & MACKAY

A MOMENT IN TIME | 183

184 | A MOMENT IN TIME

Leith A 900
Glasgow (M8)
Forth Road Bridge (A90)
Berwick upon Tweed (A1)
Omni
City Centre Attractions

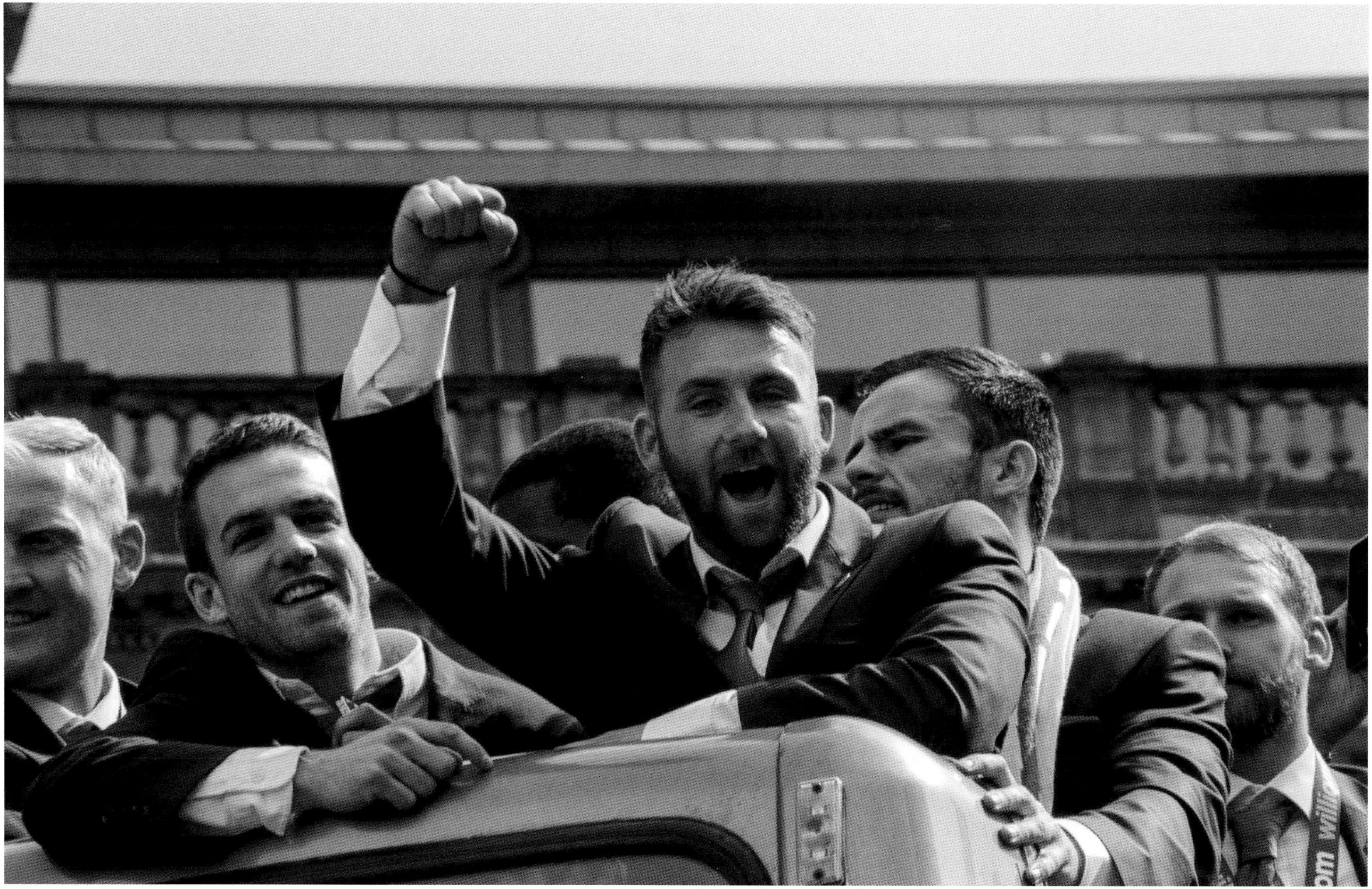

A MOMENT IN TIME | 187

188 | A MOMENT IN TIME

A MOMENT IN TIME | 189

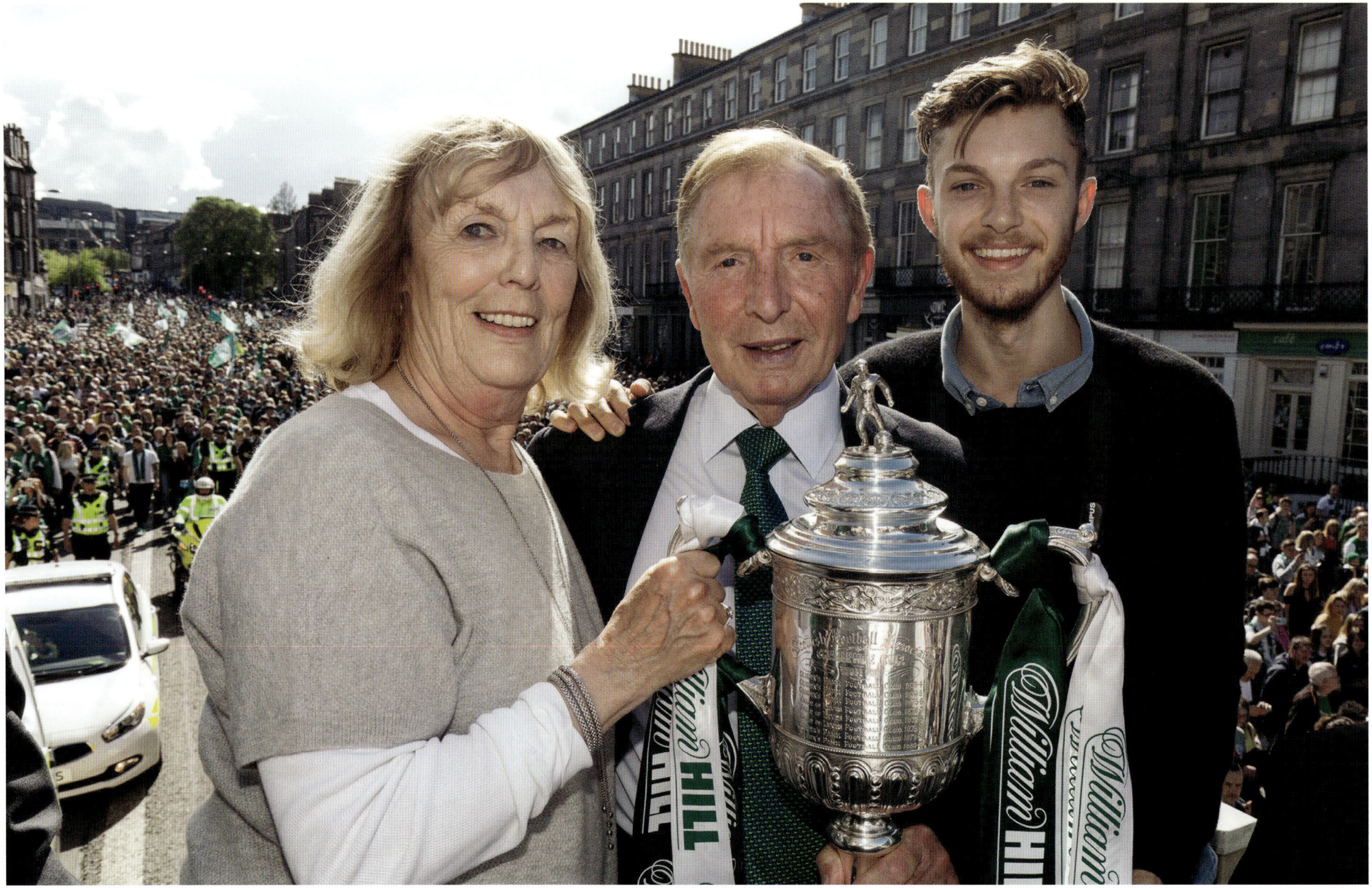
William
HILL

A MOMENT IN TIME | 191

192 | A MOMENT IN TIME

A MOMENT IN TIME | 193

194 | A MOMENT IN TIME

LAGERS, WINES & SPIRITS
LIVE SPORT
CASA AMIGA
POLICE
POLICE
POLICE

196 | A MOMENT IN TIME

A MOMENT IN TIME | 197

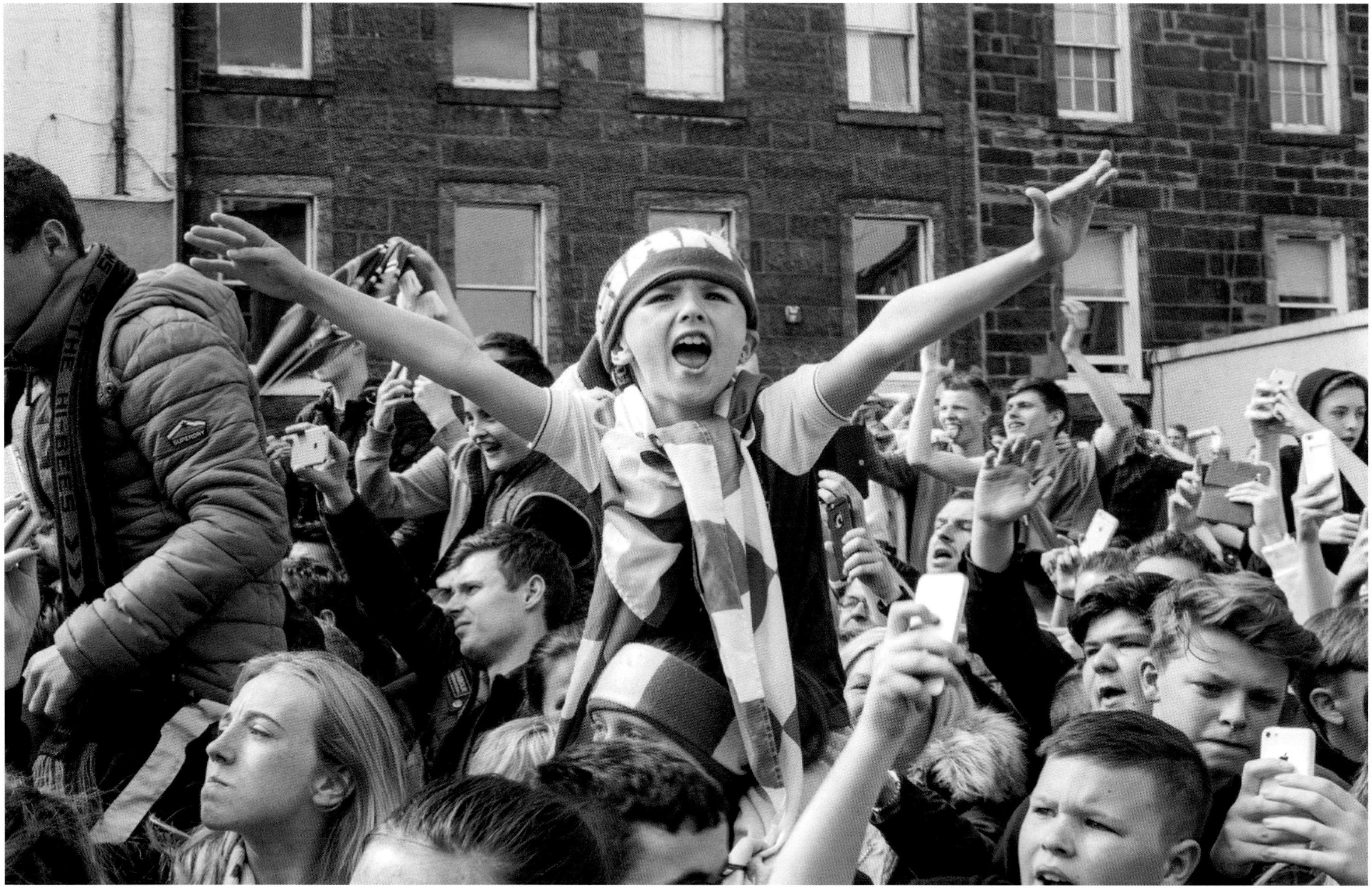

A MOMENT IN TIME | 199

GILFEDDER & McINNES
POLICE
POLICE
POLICE
SP15 YNS
SWEET SHOP
JANE STREET

HIBERNIAN
MARATHON BET
HIBERNIAN FC
SCOTTISH CUP WINNERS 2016

202 | A MOMENT IN TIME

A MOMENT IN TIME | 203

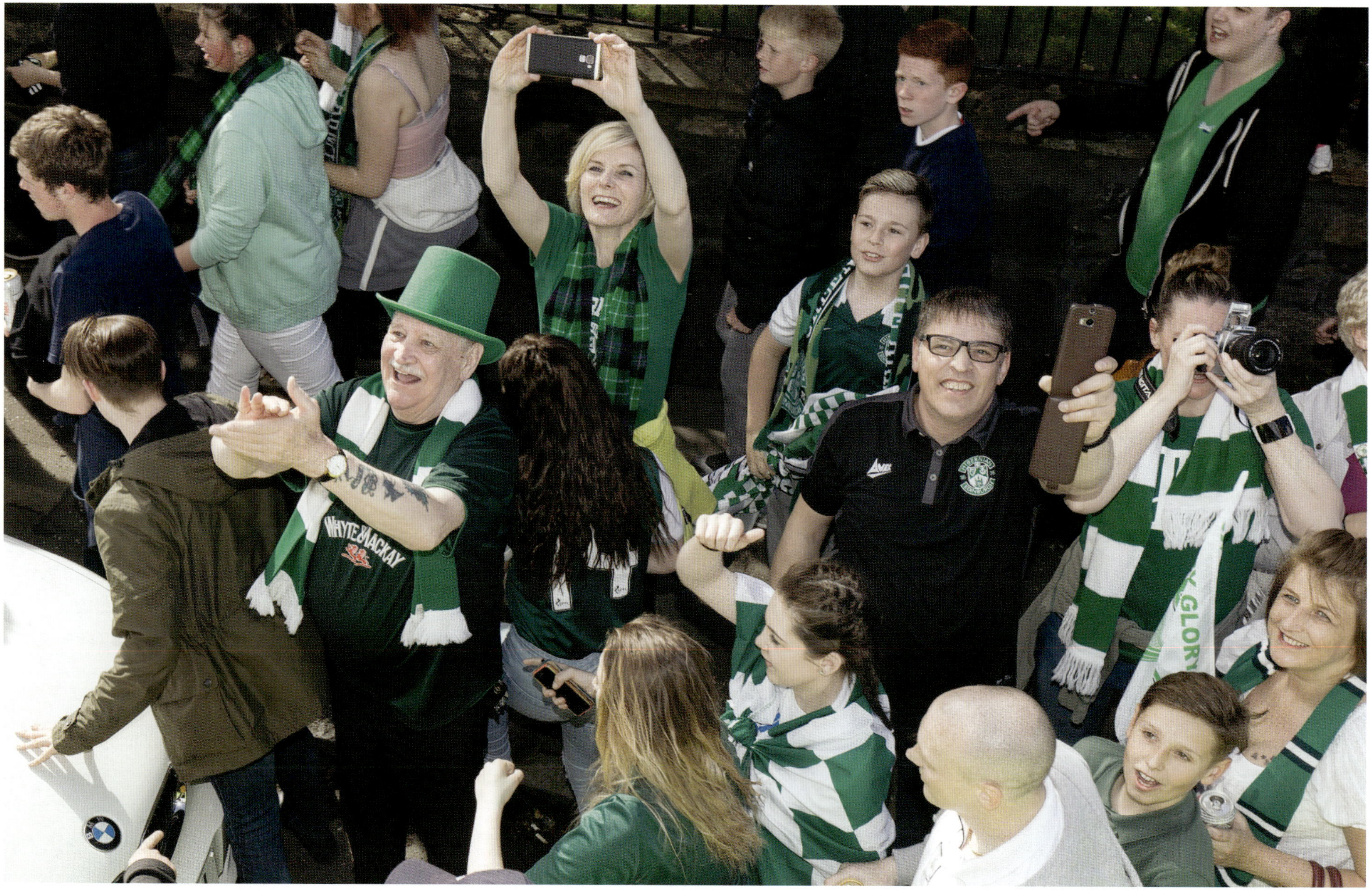
WHYTE & MACKAY
GLORY

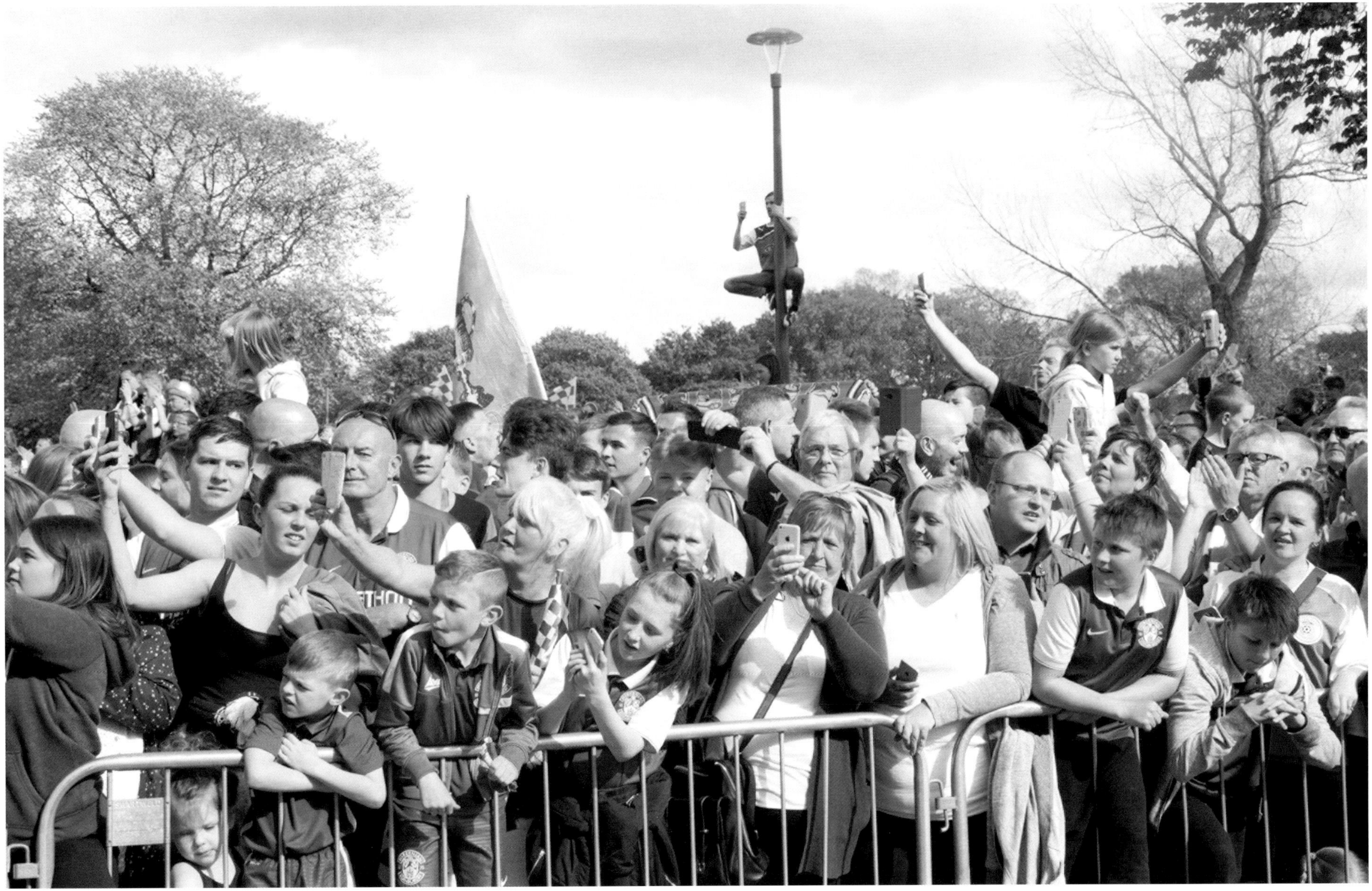

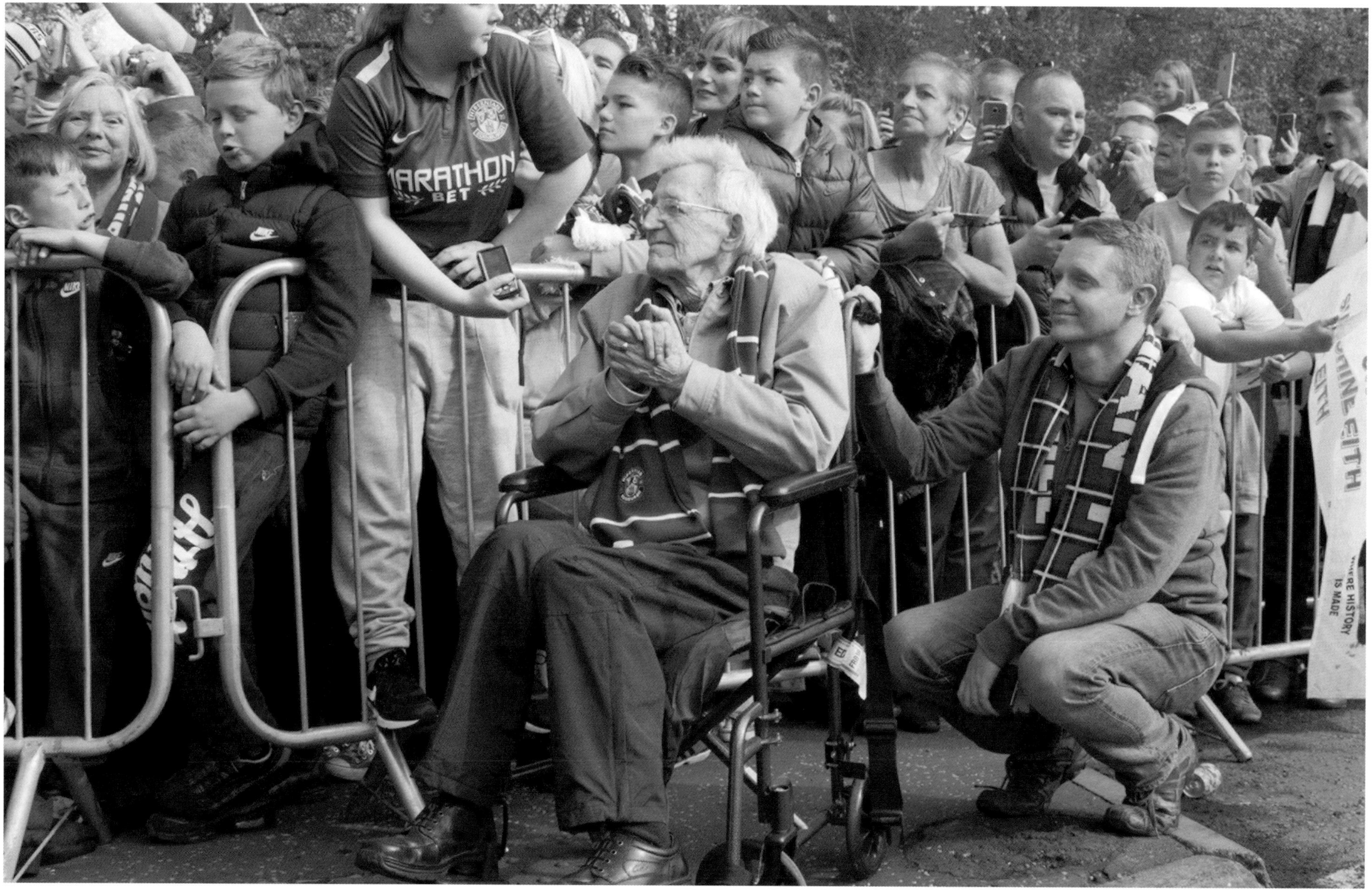
BET
IS MADE

A MOMENT IN TIME | 207

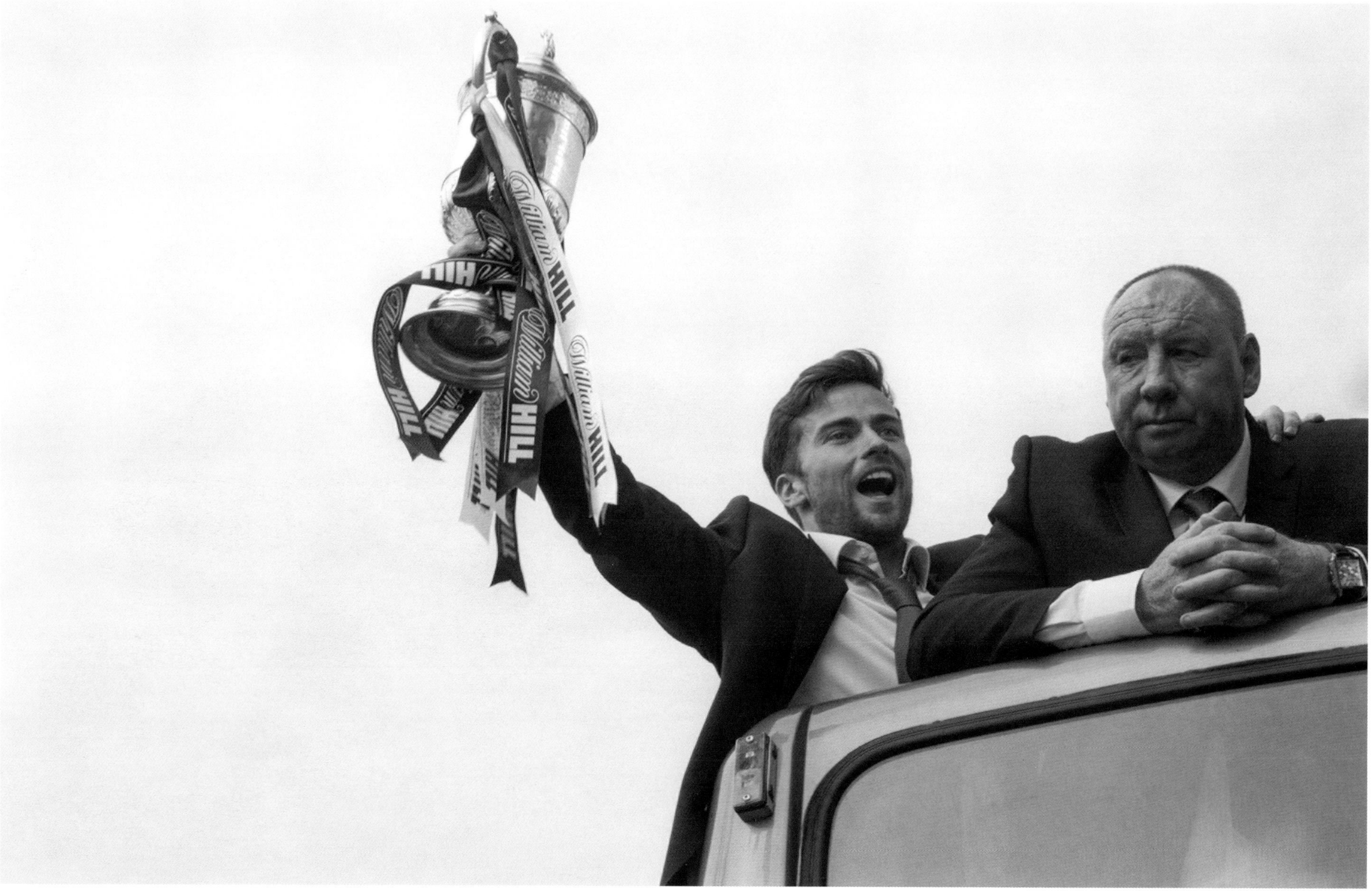
William HILL

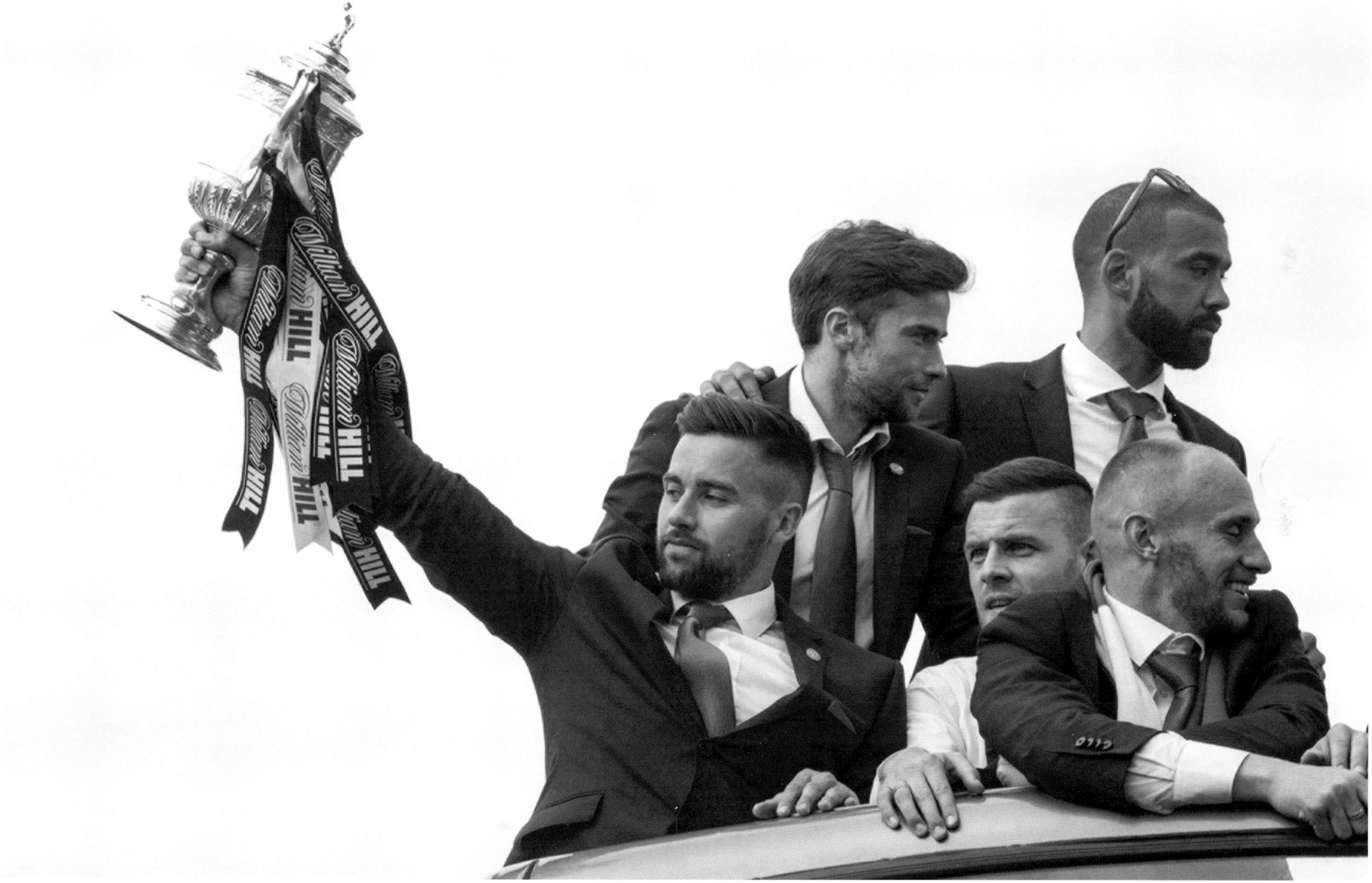
William HILL

210 | A MOMENT IN TIME

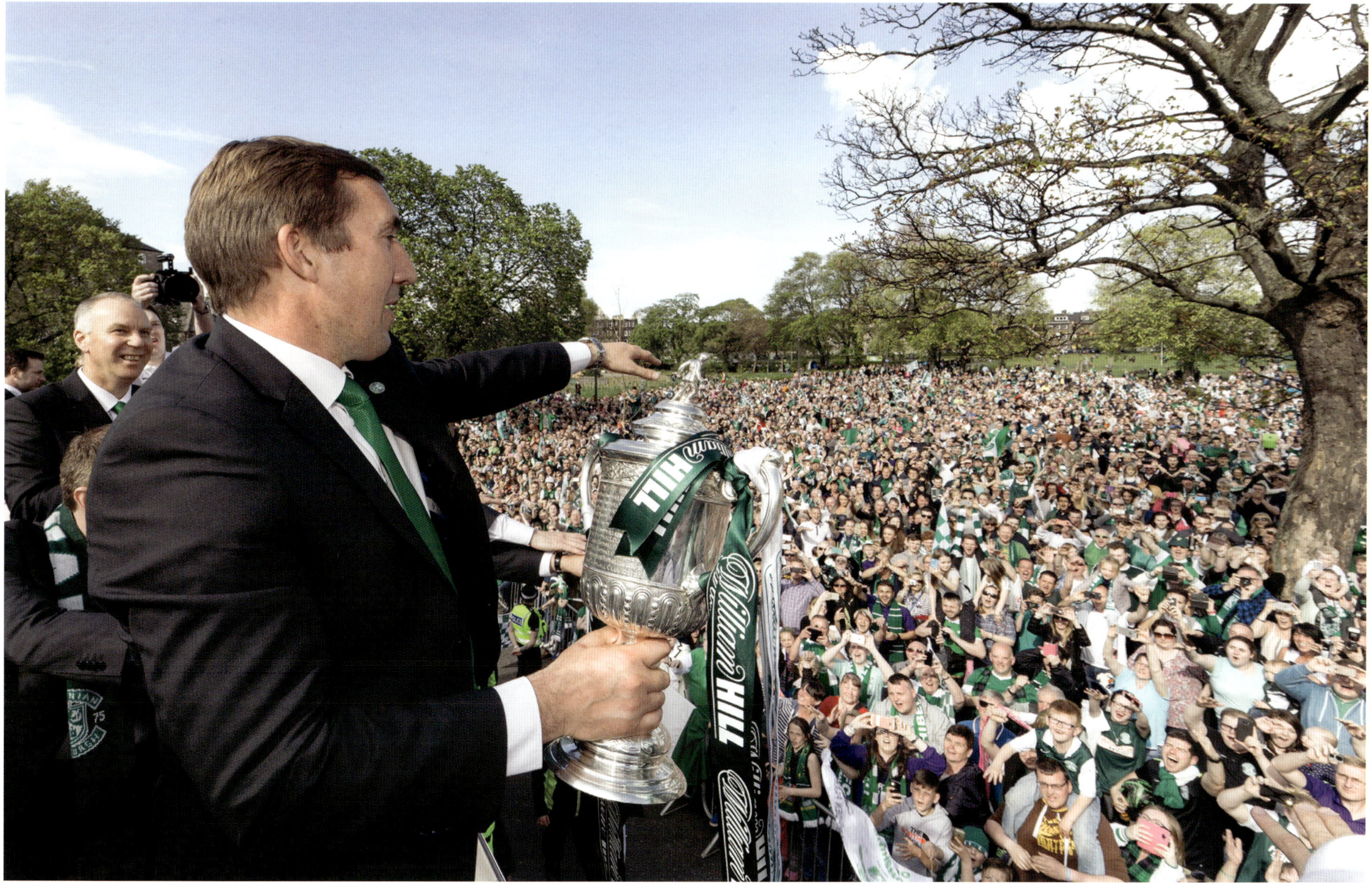
William HILL

212 | A MOMENT IN TIME

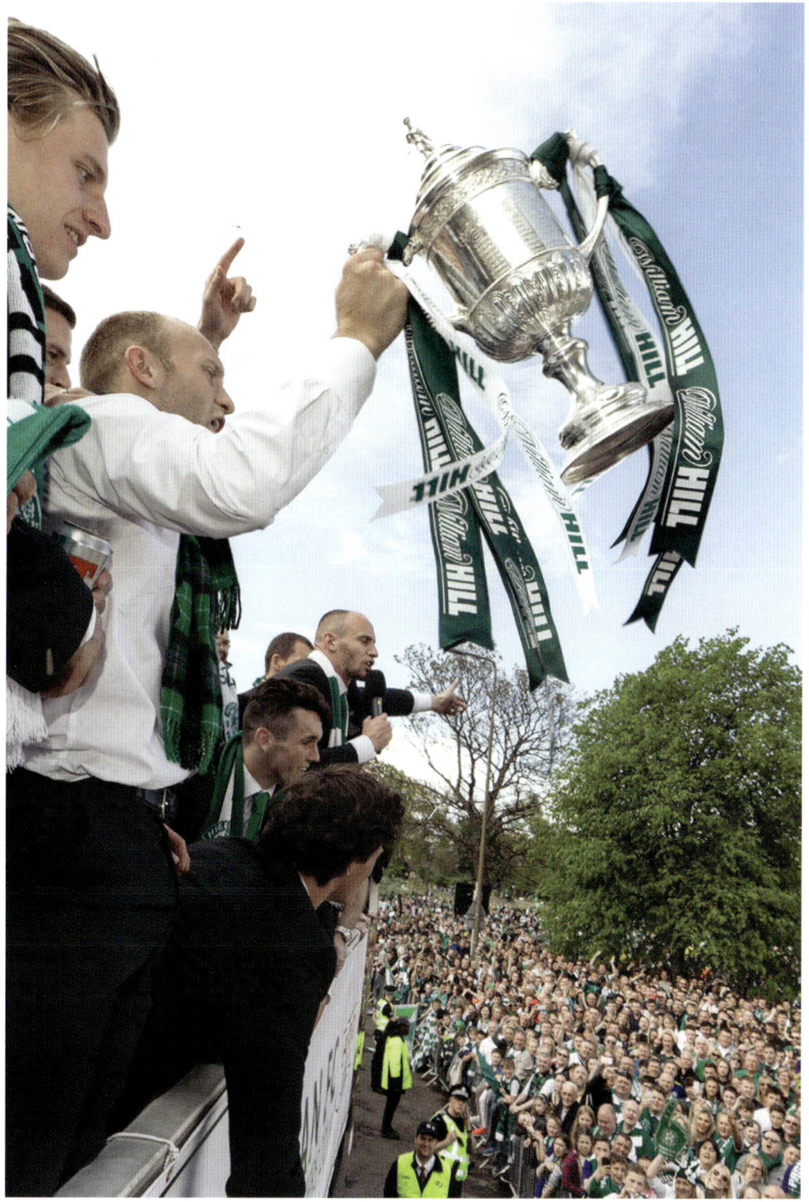
William HILL

214 | A MOMENT IN TIME

A MOMENT IN TIME | 215

216 | A MOMENT IN TIME

114 YEARS IS NO MORE

114 YEARS IS NO MORE

After ten unsuccessful attempts to have the name of Hibernian chiselled into the silver lining around a solid base of rich brown wood, the Club stood on the precipice of history on 21 May 2016.

Each passing year, optimism remained within the Hibernian support, each year the magic of the cup brought about a feeling that this year would be the year the wait would end, despite over a century of hurt.

That feeling started to grow once again when Darren McGregor, a Hibernian fan from birth, lit the long fuse towards the most spectacular explosion of green and white swamping the streets of Edinburgh ever. The defender fired in a strike from 20 yards out on 9 January 2016 at Stark's Park – the 1,000th goal the Club had scored in the history of the competition – allowing a feeling of belief from everyone connected to Hibernian to take seed.

A stirring comeback in the Edinburgh Derby against Heart of Midlothian at Tynecastle aided Hibernian's progress and belief, as did a hard-fought victory away to Inverness Caledonian Thistle just days after a late and agonising defeat to Ross County in the Scottish League Cup Final.

Debutant goalkeeper Conrad Logan produced a man of the match display against Dundee United in the semi-final at Hampden Park, with his saves during open play and in the penalty shoot-out fanning the flames of belief even more in the hunt for success, as the stars appeared to be aligning for something sensational to occur.

Heading into the William Hill Scottish Cup Final, history was already made, with both Hibernian and Rangers reaching the showpiece finale – the first time that two teams from outside the top-flight had contested the final.

A rip-roaring start saw Anthony Stokes' measured finish slide beyond Wes Foderingham's reach, before Kenny Miller equalised for Rangers and Andy Halliday's crisp drive from distance crashed into the back of the net to hand the Ibrox side the advantage in the closing 26 minutes.

With 15 minutes to go, still trailing 2-1, the Hibernian support played a crucial part, lifting the volume and the players, with their sheer determination to will the team on to a win.

In those moments it was obvious how much that it meant to the fans to see the cup won, a moment created for them, for those around them and for those no longer with them. And in what style it happened.

A Liam Henderson corner found Stokes who headed in minutes after the crowd's initial stirring and then, in injury-time, the wait was over. A whipped Henderson corner saw captain David Gray get his head on the cross, and the net bulged as the ball flew into it.

114 years of agony and pain were released. Fans remembered those who were no longer here, whilst gripping those they love close to them in euphoric celebrations, showing exactly what it meant in the history of the Club. Not only had Gray added his name to those of Patrick Lafferty and Andy McGeachan as Hibernian

players to score the winning goal in a Scottish Cup Final, but the long, long wait was ended and the supporters had their reward to savour after persevering for decade after decade.

After the curtain was drawn by the players on the 114-year long wait, an incredibly cathartic rendition of Sunshine on Leith rang out around the bowl of Hampden Park, dramatic and poignant in equal measures.

The win on that day was for the fans, all of those who had waited and endured the constant jibes and references to 1902. For those there to share the moment, who stood up and backed the team when they needed it the most, and for those unable to be there in person but who were there in spirit.

The day after the triumph, on Sunday, May 22, 150,000 supporters flooded the streets of Edinburgh and showed what it meant to our community to see history created.

21 May 2016 added another chapter to the long and rich history of Hibernian in the most dramatic of fashion – a moment in time which will never be forgotten.